Cocoa and Kinship in Ghana

Cocoa and Kinship in Ghana

The matrilineal Akan of Ghana

Christine Okali

Published for the International African Institute
by
Kegan Paul International
London, Boston and Melbourne

First published in 1983
by Kegan Paul International Ltd
39 Store Street, London WC1E 7DD,
9 Park Street, Boston, Mass. 02108, USA and
464 St Kilda Road, Melbourne,
Victoria 3004, Australia
Printed and bound in Great Britain by
Robert Hartnoll, Bodmin, Cornwall

Library of Congress Cataloging in Publication Data

Okali, C.
Cocoa and Kinship in Ghana
Bibliography: p.
Includes index.
1. Akan (African people) - Economic conditions.
2. Akan (African people) - Social life and customs.
3. Cacao - Ghana. 4. Cocoa trade - Ghana. I. Title.
DT510.43.A53O35 1983 306.8'3'09667 83-191

ISBN 0-7103-0041-7

Contents

Tables

Preface

This book is largely based on research that was carried out during the years 1971-3 and could not have been completed without the co-operation of many farmers who willingly gave their time. I am particularly indebted to Nana Asare Bediako III and Nana Kofi Kusi who made me welcome in their respective settlements, and to Mr Alex Mensah, a cocoa farmer himself, who assisted with the collection of data at Dominase.

I am grateful also for the permission given by the Institute of Statistical, Social and Economic Research, University of Ghana, Legon, to use material gathered while I was working there and for the time to write. Part of the field-work was funded by a grant administered by the Cocoa Research Co-ordinating Committee at Legon and to them also I owe many thanks.

Since starting this work I have benefited from the constant support and encouragement of my colleagues Susan Mabey and Dr C. Oppong, and I owe much to their comments on the manuscript and to those of the late Professor Fortes, Dr E.N. Goody, Professor Morton-Williams and Professor Fiawoo. I am also grateful to Valerie Dudley, who completed much of the final proof-reading. This book is, however, my own, and the sole responsibility for the end product must be mine.

Introduction

This work has two major objectives. One is to analyse the significance of customary property relations among the Akan in determining the distribution of cocoa farm ownership between persons of different age, sex and status and for the management and organisation of cocoa farms. The other is to document contemporary changes in kinship and associated changes in the economic environment.

The main theme is the management and organisation of cocoa farms among the Akan; this arose out of a more general concern with declining cocoa production in Ghana and the long-term care of cocoa trees which usually have a life-span of at least forty years. Occupational and spatial mobility (Boaten, 1974), the use of hired labour (Broatch, 1956; Uchendu, 1969), decreasing real returns to production (Leston, 1974), and the incidence of pests and diseases (Hunter, 1961; Hill, 1963; Beckett, 1972; Collingwood, 1972) had all been reported as contributing to the production decline, while questions surrounding the inheritance of farm properties among the matrilineal Akan had also been pinpointed as important variables disturbing the long-term care of farms (Okali and Kotey, 1971). This latter finding was particularly interesting in view of the rate at which cocoa production had expanded throughout the forest belt of Ghana and among the Akan. It contradicted the findings of Polly Hill (Hill, 1963) who, in detailing the expansion of cocoa in the Eastern Region, demonstrated that corporate land-owning acted as a spur to expansionary enterprise. It was these conflicting findings and the lack of studies considering cocoa production from this viewpoint (see Okali and Addy, 1974) that suggested the present work, which concentrates on variables usually categorised as non-economic - as distinct from viewing cocoa production as the result of the factor mix determined by the relative market prices of the inputs and outputs involved. Analyses from an economic viewpoint are covered elsewhere (see Kotey, Okali and Rourke, 1974; and Okali and Addy, 1974).

Underlying much of the literature on the widespread agricultural changes in West Africa, including the transfer from subsistence to cash cropping, is the assumption that certain customary principles are eroded in the process. Attention has focused on the disintegration of descent groups as a whole, especially their corporate functions, and on the emergence of the elementary family as the key kinship group with respect to economic co-operation, especially in societies characterised by matrilineal descent and inheritance. A number of writers have suggested that this is true among cocoa producers in Ghana (Busia, 1951; Woodman, 1966; Benneh, 1970; Adomako-Sarfoh, 1971). Even Hill (1963), whose main interest was in the formation of landed estates and who emphasised the persistence of customary principles of economic co-operation among matrilineal and patrilineal communities, reports that the forces of capitalist enterprise were represented by the individual farmer and his wives and children (Hill, 1963: 16). Nevertheless, as early as 1948, Fortes (1948) considered that if the lineage system held its own for another fifty years, possibly all cocoa farms would be lineage-owned in Ashanti. Clearly the introduction of cash cropping had led to changes in customary property relations in rural areas but considerably more information was needed to highlight their significance. The present work therefore seeks to investigate this link between the organisation of cash crop production and customary principles of social organisation among the matrilineal Akan.

Although cocoa has been the major source of employment, production and foreign exchange earnings in Ghana for decades, few writers have focused on the farmers themselves instead of the crop, and most studies have considered only one particular aspect of production. Hence Shepherd (1936), Nowell (1938), Watson (1948), Jibowu (1956) and Quaidoo (1956) considered the problem of the availability of cash for farming, farmer indebtedness and the pledging of farms. Killick (1966), Appiah (1970), Rourke (1971) and Addo (1972) have all concentrated on the hired labour force involved in cocoa production. Few have looked in detail at other sources of labour on farms. The distribution of returns from farms has not been considered although there has been some reference to the transfer of property between owners (Benneh, 1970; Adomako-Sarfoh, 1971; Okali and Kotey, 1971). Interest in mobile farmers has led to investigations of land purchase arrangements and demonstrated the significance of the role played by migrating farmers in the development of the industry (Hill, 1963; Adomako-Sarfoh, 1965; Benneh, 1970; Kotey, 1972). One of the earliest and most comprehensive studies of cocoa production was that of Beckett (1947) which was concerned with detailing costs and returns to farmers working within their own chiefdom or on their own stool land. ('Stool' land was land vested in the office of the chief, available to any citizen, if uncultivated.) A similar study has been completed for a migrant cocoa farming community (Okali, 1975).

This work attempts a broader view: the whole problem of the significance of property rights is viewed within a wide perspective including the acquisition and development of farms, the distribution of returns and the transfer of farms from one generation to the next. Two farming situations, one in home areas and one away, are compared. In this the work differs from previous studies that, following the approach of Polly Hill's investigations in the 1950s, have been directed towards farmers who work outside their home towns and who appear to be most involved in the market economy.

Overall, the book is related to two major fields of research.

Firstly it is relevant to the field of economic anthropology as a whole and the burning question of the pertinence of classical economic theory for interpreting economies organised by domestic groups and kinship relations (Sahlins, 1972). Secondly, it is related to the growing body of literature documenting the changing West African scene following the growth of urban areas, and the extension of Western education and resultant geographical and social mobility; it attempts to understand the process of social change itself. One of the most fascinating themes followed in these studies is the changing domestic scene and the relevance of customary kinship relationships in the modern setting, and it is to this body of work that this book is most closely related. Hence it is the economic relationships between spouses, parents and their offspring and matrikin that are investigated here.

The field material was collected between the years 1971 and 1974 and covers a number of different types of information. Thus in Chapter 3, community-level data from two contrasting work-places, at home and away, are used to introduce the theme of changing production relations through space and over the life-cycle. Information on the distribution of farm ownership among the farm population and the composition of domestic and work units is used to examine the relative strength of ties of descent, marriage and parenthood in these different localities. However, data on the structural composition of domestic and work units is inadequate for understanding the role played by different persons in the development of farms. This is achieved more by the use of case histories of actual investments made in holdings and these are presented in Chapter 4. Sources of land, labour and cash are documented along with actual time budgets of work completed on farms which have reached different stages of maturity and are owned by farmers of different sex and age groups. At this point the extent to which wives are involved in their own separate economic activities is considered. It can be seen that no one pattern persists throughout a lifetime and indeed it is the changing relations with different categories of persons that is most significant.

Court records are used to highlight attempts to claim rights not customarily defined, and to evaluate the security of all claims, including the corporate claims of matrikin, which are not necessarily based on assistance given. Material collected from a group of farmers in Ashanti follows.

The findings are reviewed in Chapter 6 and discussed in terms of the interrelationship between customary norms and behaviour patterns and the way in which cocoa farms are operated. The book concludes with a discussion of the persistence of traditional values in contemporary economic settings.

Chapter 1

Economic change and kinship relationships

Considerable work has now been done throughout the world investigating changes in family patterns. A feature noted in other parts of the world is the increasing importance of conjugal relationships in the face of the declining importance of ties of consanguinity. There have been a number of urban studies in Africa observing continuity and change in systems of kinship and marriage reviewed in UNESCO (1956), Little (1959), Southall (1961), Aldous (1962), Simms (1965) and Bott (1971). The educated elite has been the focus of a number of such works (Smythe and Smythe, 1960; Lloyd, 1966; Oppong, 1970). Both urban migration and education have therefore been clearly pinpointed as important variables affecting these relationships, although, overall, modern changes in kinship have been linked with wider economic changes in general.

RURAL AREAS

Few writers have compared rates and effects of changes in urban and rural areas (defined according to population size) except to observe that urban areas are frequently at the spearhead of any changes going on elsewhere (Goode, 1963). However, a number of authors have observed changes in kinship systems in rural areas in Africa and identified societies experiencing different rates of change. Some attempt has also been made to specify particular aspects of the economic scene that have acted as important stimuli to ongoing changes in family systems.

Organised groups of kin such as descent groups have been noted as being particularly susceptible to economic variables. Fortes writes that 'Unilineal descent groups break down when a modern economic framework with occupational differentiation linked to a wide range of specialised skills, to productive capital and to monetary media of exchange, is introduced' (Fortes, 1953: 24). Gough (1961), stressing the Marxist preconception about the paramountcy of the control of means of production over anything else in governing patterns of social organisation, states that the gradual incorporation of society into a unitary market system is the root cause of modern kinship change. Goody (1965) is more cautious and notes in addition change in political functions, customarily performed by the widest span of the lineage. Thus he notes that the disappearance of unilineal descent groups is linked with the growth of economic and social individualism, where persons tend to have direct political and economic ties with political and economic agencies, rather than through multifunctional units such as kin groups. He suggests that once descent groups no longer provide rights to means of production, which are linked further with the amount and type of property to be inherited, they, along with other customary units of co-operation, lose their importance. Hopen (1958), Gough (1952) and Goody (1962) all suggest that descent groups and what Gough describes as 'primitive grouping based on birth' are incompatible with social and spatial mobility, especially the latter.

Although similar changes can be observed in all societies, matriliny is widely reported to be particularly subject to change (Schneider and Gough, 1961). Gough (1961) links descent systems with levels of productivity and questions whether there is some productivity height at which some form of bilateral or patrilineal system emerges as a result of the matrilineage or lineage segment no longer being the unit of joint ownership of property. Goody (1962) mentions the disintegrating effect of large differences in wealth, since inequalities upset the operation of equal exchange to distant uterine kin made in recognition of reciprocal ties between these groups. Other writers suggest that it is pressure on available productive resources that makes matriliny less viable (Colson, 1960; Allan, 1965; Douglas, 1969; Goody, 1969), although Turner (1957) writes that wide-span local matrilineages tend to be found where access to land or other valuable natural resources is limited and, like Gray and Gulliver (1964), observes that extended matrilineages tend to be associated with the possession of fixed estates.

Douglas (1969) is also less concerned with documenting the inevitable doom of matriliny than with stressing its viability compared with patriliny, during periods of economic expansion. She concludes that matriliny, by not providing a strong authority structure and by being flexible, allows the enterprising individual to override ascribed rules in these situations.

A major change identified among societies practising matrilineal inheritance and descent is the tendency of the elementary family, consisting of a man, his wife/wives and their offspring, to become the most important basis of economic co-operation (Gough, 1952; Turner, 1957). In these and similar studies, it is being observed among matrilineal societies that the male line is increasingly taking precedence over the female, but everywhere lineages are found to be losing strength.

PROPERTY RIGHTS

Attention has been drawn particularly to changes in the use of customary methods of transmitting property rights, although few suggest that inheritance rules themselves have changed. The property rights of persons, other than those of the descent group, hinge therefore on the ability of individuals to gain direct access to resources and thus to acquire personal as distinct from corporate property. Richards (1939), writing of the Bemba, observes that personal property acquired by a man's own efforts may go to sons, wives and sisters rather than to customary heirs. She noted, however, that traditionally there were few inheritable goods and that it is money, a new form of wealth, which is divided among a man's own children rather than his nephews. A similar point is made by Turner (1957): farmers are retaining money earned from their cash crops for the use of themselves and their own elementary families with whom they are founding farms. Individuals are recorded by Gough (1952) to be even surrendering their rights in ancestral property to their sisters while acquiring new lands to be given to their wives and children, and among the Yakö, matrilineal ties are being undermined by successful claims of sons to their fathers' personal possessions and by the retention of marriage payments by fathers (Forde, 1950). Finally, Goody (1962), while noting that methods of circumventing descent group claims by giving gifts inter vivos of personally acquired property between fathers and sons are not new, points out that the scarcer productive resources become, and the more intensively they are used, the greater the tendency towards the retention of these resources within the basic productive and reproductive unit - which in the large majority of cases is the elementary family.

Other means of circumventing rather than changing customary rules have also been observed. Forde (1950) notes the increasing occurrence of marriage between members of the same matriclan by which means a man's own sons are regarded as his matrilineal heirs. Like Goody, he hesitates to regard this behaviour as entirely new since the secret hiding of movable wealth by fathers and sons had frequently been reported in the past.

Several writers, whether reporting on matrilineal or patrilineal descent groups, have written of changes or pressures towards change with respect to the rights of women to economic resources, particularly land. The dispersal of land through both sexes is regarded by Goody (1970), for instance, as being virtually incompatible with the formation of localised unilineal descent groups.

Dupire (1971), describing women among the Fulani WoDaabe, pastoral nomads of Niger, observes actual changes in the law of inheritance that are all oriented towards the dispersal of the family patrimony which, by its very nature, should exclude transmission through females. Nevertheless, Fulani women are progressively acquiring more and more extended rights, and first and foremost by virtue of membership of their patrilineage.

Most of these studies suggest close working relationships between spouses and offspring in modern economic settings, and hence the desire of men in matrilineal societies to strengthen these bonds. Boserup (1970) is one of the few who concentrates on the changing rights of women as independent cultivators, and observes that women in Africa south of the Sahara are losing these rights and may eventually become unpaid helpers on their husbands' land. Galletti, Baldwin and Dina (1956), on the other hand, suggest that some women are unlikely to place themselves in this disadvantageous position. Thus Yoruba women refused to assist their husbands on cocoa farms without receiving payment.

KINSHIP AND CASH CROP PRODUCTION

The all-pervading aspect of kinship in traditional settings in Africa is a constant theme in anthropological works, and here the organisation of the economic system has been shown to be closely related to kinship variables. Nevertheless there are few detailed studies of the importance of kinship for the actual operation of modern agricultural enterprises; most look for specific changes per se and treat economic activities as being interrelated with other activities rather than opposed to them. Long's work in Zambia (Long, 1968) and that of Parkin (1972) in Kenya are exceptional. Using the case study approach, Long discusses the value of expertise and finance from relatives and friends to potential cash crop farmers and notes the ensuing friction when these same farmers are established and no longer in need of assistance. He also refers to changes in the organisation of agricultural labour, settlement patterns, residential groupings and attitudes towards landholding. Of particular interest in Long's work is his reference to the significance of role performance for creating property rights. Thus he reports that in settling disputes between matrilineal kinsmen and sons over succession, the deciding factor was who had contributed most to the development of the farms.

Parkin (1972), discussing the Giriama of Kenya who grow coconut palms for copra, observes that elders mediate in claims based on agnatic ancestry but also act as witnesses to land and palm transactions that make no reference to agnatic relatedness and clanship but which are based on sale or mortgage. Thus again features of modernity appear to be sustaining the traditional power of the elders although Parkin concludes that change will inevitably follow from the new sources of economic and political power that are being concentrated in the hands of the young.

A number of authors have referred to a negative relationship between successful entrepreneurial developments and the fulfilment of kinship obligations. Thus one of the rules of planned farms in Central Africa was that only the immediate family of the owner was permitted to reside on a holding since the fulfilment of kinship obligations resulted in the splitting of farms into uneconomic units (Allan, 1965). Lanfranchi (1962), writing of cocoa farmers in the Ivory Coast, states emphatically the bearing of matriliny on the care of cocoa farms

> in certain regions, the system of matrilinear succession under which the young man, since he is not his father's heir, has no more to gain from the prosperity of the plantation than a nephew, who is his uncle's heir and is not interested in the income during the uncle's lifetime, is the obstacle to management on a family basis. (p. 68)

THE GHANAIAN SCENE

The literature for Ghana covering changes and strains towards change in kinship and marriage and associated property relationships, particularly among cocoa farmers, is similar to literature for other countries. Frequently cocoa production itself is pinpointed as the most important factor leading to change. Thus Fortes (1973), writing of the matrilineal Ashanti, notes conflicts following the exploitation of land for commercial purposes - over rights of alienation and mortgage on the one hand and rights of family ownership and of inheritance and succession on the other. Earlier he reported that the volume of witchcraft accusations in Ashanti was increasing as claims based on lineage ties came to be felt more onerous (Fortes, 1950). Field (1960) expresses concern over the extent of insecurity and anxiety caused by contentions over money and cocoa farm inheritance in rural areas in southern Ghana.

Much of the evidence concerning the declining importance of ties of descent has again revolved around transfers of self-acquired cocoa property to wives and offspring (Fortes, 1948; Meek, 1957; Benneh, 1970; Adomako-Sarfoh, 1971). Field (1960) observes that self-acquired property, with the individual's right to dispose of it as he likes, has undermined the status of family-owned property with its inherent heavy kinship obligations.

Other writers have referred to a narrowing of the generation depth and span of the affective matrilineage. Fortes (1948) writes that inheritance among the matrilineal Ashanti was already in 1948 becoming restricted to the closest kin, the matrilineal issue of a man's own mother and her sisters. Danquah (1928) - writing earlier - and Banneh (1970), commenting on the Akan as a whole, report a similar tendency. Benneh (1970) observes in particular the increasing rights of women; sisters can inherit cocoa farms from a deceased brother, even though in former times a male relative, a nephew or cousin, would have been chosen as a successor.

Few detailed studies exist of changing work roles within agriculture and there are conflicting views about the independent role played by women in cocoa production. Both Field (1960) and Boserup (1970) note the traditional role of Ashanti and Akim males as warriors, and females as subsistence producers. Field reports a persistence of the female preoccupation with subsistence farming but comments that the women of rural Ghana are economically independent, most producing more than their consumption requirements. Kyerematen (1973), however, observes that Ashanti women grow food crops for home consumption alone while Hill (1962) reports that in New Juaben and certain native Akim areas, about half the women are cocoa farmers in their own right.

Fortes (1950) is one of the few who refers to economic co-operation between spouses and the resultant insecurity of women. Thus he notes the increasing tendency among the Ashanti for matrilineal heirs to eject their predecessors' widows and children from the enjoyment of properties that they helped to build, and as a result the fact that women prefer to work for themselves as an insurance against the future rather than to assist their husbands. Again, therefore, it is not the changing of customary principles that is emphasised but rather ways of circumventing these.

Disadvantages of both patrilineal and matrilineal kinship obligations for the actual operation of business enterprises have also been mentioned. The observation of patrilineal rules of inheritance among Anlo Ewe shallot farmers is reported to have led to excessive fragmentation of farm plots, making it impossible for the small farmers to reap much from the land even though it gives some security to all members of the lineage (Benneh, 1971). As early as 1923, Rattray was writing that matriliny cramps individual effort by its 'unnatural' mode of inheritance (Rattray, 1923: 237-8), while Okali and Kotey (1971) pinpointed a number of problems connected with the transfer of farms from one generation to the next according to matrilineal rules of inheritance, all of which result in the neglect of farms. Garlick (1971), writing of Kumasi traders, is less adamant and comments that objections to matrilineal succession are part of a wider complaint about responsibilities in life. He suggests, however, that some of the problems of Akan businessmen could be related to matrilineal inheritance since 'A trader's successor rarely knew anything about the business, and his aim was to realize the assets as soon as possible' (Garlick, 1971: 88). He suggests that this raises fewer problems for cocoa farmers since their skills are more widely known.

Hill (1963) uses case material to look at the organisation of cocoa production and, as observed earlier, does not stress change or the harmful effects of kinship connections for the operation of holdings. Thus she writes that there is 'no evidence that the enterprising individual was hampered by matrilineage or patrilineage or that the lineage forms themselves underwent modification' (Hill, 1963: 16). Her case histories also present no evidence of whole enterprises being distributed according to personal choice. Similarly Fortes (1950), in spite of his reference to changes, when reporting actual field data warns against exaggerating degrees of change, and in 1950 wrote that although the solidarity of the maximal lineage had declined in matters of a personal or domestic nature, the strength of matrilineal kinship, within the constellation of kinship ties in the domestic group, remained unchanged. Thus he notes that only a minority of men take care to provide for their wives and children by making samansew, (1) and three out of four cocoa farms pass from one generation to the next by matrilineal inheritance (1950: 272). Van de Geest (1974), in his study of a Kwahu lineage, also reports no case of a man rewarding his wife with samansew. Nevertheless, Brokensha (1966) and Woodman (1966) suggest that in conflicts arising over property rights, the extent to which help has been received from others is a deciding factor, indicating that wives and offspring may not need to rely solely on gifts for assistance given, since the courts are themselves introducing changes in property rights.

CONTINUITY AND CHANGE

Overall, the literature on the subject of changes in systems of marriage and kinship and the relationship between business activi-

---

1 'Deathbed declaration'. Customarily, a man who is seriously ill can dispose of his self-acquired property by making such a declaration. It is made with as much publicity as possible and the recipient must provide drink, aseda, to signify his acceptance. Ownership is not transferred until the death of the owner.

ties and kinship variables displays an agreement that there has been a breakdown of organised groups of kin owing to various economic changes in rural communities both in Ghana and elsewhere. The division of labour, the monetisation of exchange, economic individualism, the incorporation of societies into a unitary market system and actual changes in productivity have all been mentioned as features of the economy linked with change. Most of these imply that the basic independent variable is the ability of the individual to operate without reference to descent groups. In farming communities, this refers in particular to individuals having independent access to land, labour and expertise.

Quantifiable evidence of change among matrilineal societies relies heavily on statements about changes in property transfers, from inheritance to gifts to non-customary heirs. In particular, the increasing importance of offspring, wives and females as a whole has been mentioned, and emphasis placed on their rights with respect to the means of production following the elementary family's emergence as the most important basis of economic co-operation. Conflicts of rights and claims among descent groups have been referred to, even if changes in property transfers have not. On the other hand, few writers have looked at the changing position of individuals over their lifetimes. In this book an attempt is made to do this; it does, for instance, look at women in roles other than that of wife.

Some of the studies of societies practising matrilineal systems of descent and inheritance have suggested a shift to a patrilineal or bilateral system, emphasising changes in the importance of different kin rather than a weakening of wider ties.

Moving from studies concerned with broad structural changes in societies to those looking at particular events or activities and the actual operation of business concerns, there is considerable consensus that customary kinship norms are still relevant and affect behaviour patterns and, in some cases, have been reinforced. Wider kin groups are reported as being important sources of inputs for entrepreneurial development. Thus Handwerker (1973) found that traders in Monrovia wanted to maintain kinship ties and acknowledged both the advantages and disadvantages of this pattern of living. The works of Hill (1963), Long (1968), Garlick (1971) and Parkin (1972) all suggest the need to detail the actual operation of businesses and to consider all sources of input, including land, labour, capital, management and property transfer, in order to understand the role of kinship in the modern setting. In taking this approach, the work of Oppong (1972) among the educated elite in Ghana is also significant. She emphasises the need to distinguish between particular norms and activities for men and women rather than to talk of an overall preference for a certain type of relationship between spouses, in order to understand fully the areas in which change is actually occurring.

Economic relationships may vary in different ecological settings and most writers concentrating on the Ghana cocoa farmer have focused their attention on farmers working in areas away from home. Spatial mobility has been referred to only briefly in the literature review, and among studies of social change it is mentioned most within the context of rural/urban migration. A number of authors have however emphasised the significance of length of settlement of cultivators for determining differences in matrilineal societies, and these are discussed in detail by Gough (1961). Overall, mobility is seen to limit the formation of deep localised lineages, since these cannot easily act as corporate groups if members never meet to conduct their affairs. Nevertheless Bott (1971), in her review of the variables that have been shown to be correlated with kinship relationships in various parts of the world, emphasises that even in situations of geographical dispersal, where there is greater jointness in the husband/wife relationship, ties with parents and siblings remain strong.

Lineage strength has also been linked with the mode of post-marital residence of spouses, since the residential composition of household units sets definite limits on the categories of kin and affines who may regularly and normally co-operate in the performance of various tasks. Turner (1957) writes that a fully developed ramified lineage system requires, among other conditions for its growth, that the mode of post-marital residence should be consistent with the mode of descent; a system of matrilineages requires uxorilocal marriage. However, matriliny can and does survive under different residential arrangements. Virilocal marriage is the norm among the Ndembu (Turner, 1957); the Bemba are described as being basically uxorilocal, but where a person lives is reported to depend partly on individual choice and rank (Richards, 1951). The Akan are characterised as having duo-local residence of spouses with, traditionally, consanguines residing together, although Fortes (1950) notes that the ideal of the Ashanti men is for marriage and the domestic group to be patrilocal. Goody (1965) reports that residence with the wife's kin is the most common arrangement among matrilineal peoples but comments that rarely are residential arrangements found in pure form; different patterns predominate depending on such factors as the position in the development cycle of the domestic group, order in the sibling group and relative status between husband and wife. Thus, again, conflicting views of the significance of these two particular variables suggest the need for further investigation.

Chapter 2

Method of approach

Barth (1967) has demonstrated that change can be handled more easily by looking at social behaviour as allocations of time and resources, rather than by presenting a statistical view of the practice of customs. He asks 'Is a breach of custom an event of change?' and suggests that even if a rate of breaches of custom is given, it still tells nothing about the probability or imminence of change in the custom, or about the direction of change that frequent breaches signal.

In pursuing the theme of the interrelationship between customary norms of economic relations and cocoa farming, a dynamic approach is used in this book and a model of action incorporating mobility and the life-cycle as intervening variables has been chosen. The main focus of the study is Akan cocoa farmers and, in order to place the data in perspective and consider the framework of analysis, it is necessary to give an outline of the customary property rights among the Akan and cocoa farmers in general.

THE MATRILINEAL AKAN

The population of Ghana consists of numerous ethnic groups and out of a total population of 6,632,990 in 1960, 44.1 per cent were classified as Akan. (1) The Akan thus constitute a significant proportion of the population.

The Akan occupy most of the southern half of Ghana including the western part of the Volta Region. Although they were never politically united until they came under the rule of the British colonial government, they have a common culture. Much of the literature on the Akan refers to the Ashanti, the most numerous of the Akan-speaking peoples, whose social organisation is described by Radcliffe-Brown (1950) as being the nearest approach to pure mother-right in Africa. Most recent studies of the Akan social system, and in par-

---

1 Following government policy, no reference to ethnic composition of the population is made in published data for the 1970 population census.

ticular of the Ashanti, lean heavily on the work of Sarbah (1897), Rattray (1923, 1929), Danquah (1928), Fortes (1950) and Busia (1951).

The Akan social system is characterised by matrilineal succession to political office, inheritance of property and descent. Matrilineal descent is the basis of a localised lineage organisation that is generalised through the social system as a whole by an organisation of eight dispersed clans. A maximal lineage is regarded as the local branch of these exogamous clans. Every person of free matrilineal descent is a member of his mother's lineage and hence a lineage consists of the male and female descendants of a single ancestress, descent being reckoned in the uterine line.

Every maximal lineage has a fixed home in a particular chiefdom and lineage members are citizens of this chiefdom. A citizen is therefore identified by political and kinship criteria, and strangers are by definition non-citizens in the local political community in which they are resident (Fortes, 1975). Traditionally it was possible for slaves, who were regarded as kinless, to be adopted into a lineage in a quasi-filial status and thereby attain a status, not of citizenship, but distinct from that of a stranger. Free strangers of Akan origin can never become citizens of a host community since they never cease being a citizen of their natal community. They can be incorporated, however, by being accepted as an attached element of a local lineage of their home clan by extension of the rule of clan unity. Fortes (1975) describes the population of Ahafo by migrating Akan, who formed new political communities by the fusion of clan fragments from different areas. They nevertheless remained strangers to the Ahafo host communities although they both were citizens of the Ashanti Union and subjects of the king. This situation of stranger Akan can be distinguished from that of non-Akans who are debarred from being assimilated into the host community even in a client or other dependent status (Fortes, 1975).

The most important distinction between citizens and strangers, whether Akan or non-Akan, is that of differences in cultivation rights. A citizen has the right to cultivate land vested in the office of the chief, 'stool' land, not previously occupied by anyone else (Fortes, 1975). Citizens' rights to land became of critical importance as the cultivation of cocoa spread throughout southern Ghana since they paid no purchase price, rent or tribute to either individuals or the community as represented by the chief and his council, although Adomako-Sarfoh (1965) reports that Akan strangers paid less for acquiring cultivation rights than their non-Akan counterparts. The Akan make a clear distinction between the soil and its use. The soil is vested in the chief or stool and the individual has no right to it, only the right of usufruct. Thus Ollennu (1962) describes unsufructuary title to land as the right of the individual citizen to the enjoyment of cultivation rights and even to the right of transmitting his individual enjoyment either by gift, will or inheritance, to others. It is these same usufructuary rights that are being extended to stranger farmers when reference is made to the 'purchase' of cultivation rights or land.

Though all political offices, including kingship, are vested in maximal lineages formed by reference to the greatest depth of generations and the widest span of the lineage, ownership of land and economic functions and opportunities in general are commonly vested in a segment of such a lineage equivalent to a depth of rarely more than four or five generations. This segment, which has no appointed head, usually consists of the uterine descendants of an ancestress, not more than four, occasionally five, generations antecedent to its living members, and in practice inheritance is restricted to this segment (Fortes, 1950). However, all jural transactions and arrangements within the lineage require the assent of the whole lineage community which appoints a head, abusuapanyin, to watch over its interests. Succession to this position, as in other matrilineal societies, although following the female line, is not automatic. Fortes (1950) describes the system among the Ashanti where the lineage head is chosen from among all the living male members and by a consensus of the whole body of members of both sexes. Personal qualities of tact, leadership, intelligence and knowledge of affairs determine the choice. Among his numerous duties as representative of the corporate interests of the lineage, the head formally approves the heir of a deceased member. In general a man's property may be inherited according to the following order: brothers according to seniority; own sister's son; sister's daughter's sons; mother's sister's son. In practice, however, a man's likely heir is his sister's son because of the tendency of the line of inheritance to be limited to the children of a man's mother and sister. A woman's property is handed over to the deceased's mother who will often waive her right in favour of the dead woman's relatives as follows: sisters in order of seniority; daughters, sister's daughters and grand-daughters.

The problem with the acquisition of corporate property or what is more commonly referred to as 'family property' is that the lineage or lineage segment can only function through its individual members who are themselves capable of acquiring property in their own right (Woodman, 1966). The definition of family property needs therefore to be clarified further since much of the evidence in the literature concerning changes in systems of inheritance rests on this distinction.

Some authors argue that private property does not exist or is only a temporary state of affairs. Rattray writes 'private property today was tomorrow again bound with fetters apparently unbreakable in the hands of the heir' (Rattray, 1929: 334). There is only one category of property that can easily be identified as family property: that which has been inherited and which from that point is managed by the lineage as a corporate body through the lineage head or representative.

One fundamental rule is that, upon the death intestate of a person, his self-acquired property becomes family property (Bentsi-Enchill, 1964: 126). (2) An individual may, however, make gifts of self-acquired property to non-heirs and the way in which this

2 One category of wives and children of Akan husbands have a right to inherit a portion should the husband die intestate: those subject to the provisions of the Marriage Ordinance of 1884 whereby a widow is entitled to two-ninths of her deceased husband's estate; Busia (1951) refers to similar forms of succession in Christian communities (p. 37).

property was acquired has been used to distinguish it from a family concern. Thus Bentsi-Enchill (1964) writes that family property is that which is acquired by the joint labour of two or more members of a descent group or by contributions from these members. Self-acquired property, in contrast, is that which a person acquires through his own expertise, without any help or assistance from his ancestral or family property, or by gift to himself personally. Ollennu (1962), on the other hand, observes that monies which individuals receive as their share of the proceeds of family property are regarded by custom as the individual property of each member and notes further that contributions by lineage members must be substantial or property will remain individual property. Hence Woodman (1966) finds from his analysis of judgments in court that self-acquired land does not necessarily become family land by the owner being kind enough to allow some of his matrikin to live on it and enjoy the use of it, although final decisions depend to some extent on stated or implied agreements. Bentsi-Enchill (1964) points out that the courts, in taking such decisions, are not following the doctrine of customary law, which is that even the slightest contribution creates joint rights. It is interesting in this connection to note a further comment by Woodman (1966) that a lineage head may, like a chief, be required to keep his personal property separate from the corporate property under the sanction of losing by merger any that he does not keep separate. This supports the view that even the holding of both inherited and personally acquired property at the same time by either the head or the successor to family property might lead to complications of ownership since it is difficult to prove that the funds have not been mixed (Bentsi-Enchill, 1964: 186).

As noted briefly in Chapter 1, means of avoiding conflicting conjugal, parental and matrilineal ties are not new phenomena among matrilineal groups. Cross-cousin marriage is frequently referred to as a means of assimilating these different ties, and the giving of gifts of personally acquired wealth to non-heirs, a means of avoiding descent group claims altogether. The fact that such transactions are accepted customarily does not however mean that an individual is free to make such gifts without the approval of other members of the descent group. Busia (1951) points to changes in customary procedure and mentions in particular controversies arising from descent group members refusing to acknowledge such gifts. As a result of such anomalies the Ashanti Confederacy Council in 1942 declared that where a gift was made before accredited witnesses, whether the relatives of the donor approved or not, it became valid (Busia, 1951: 37). However, only the private property of an individual can be disposed of by gift and even then it is not clear exactly how much can be given. Actual formalities associated with gift giving are also not well established (Woodman, 1966) and even the courts, often the final arbiters in disputes today, have no clearly defined legal statement of customary principles; judges refer to texts that they regard as authorities and to decisions of the superior courts. Nevertheless, most statements of customary procedure record that gifts of self-acquired property are not valid unless made with the consent of the donor's lineage and confirmed by an aseda payment from the beneficiary to them.

Although it may be argued that individual and corporate rights in property including farms are acquired by virtue of contributions made, not all persons can acquire such rights. Offspring and wives, who may form part of the unit actually working on the property, have no beneficial rights in it. Even though a wife may have laboured to help her husband to acquire and maintain property such as a house or farm, it is legally the sole possession of the husband (Sarbah, 1897; Ollennu, 1962). Wives and children do however have rights of maintenance both during a man's lifetime and after his death. After death this responsibility rests with the heir.

Because matrikin have a right to inherit property of a deceased person to the exclusion of the spouse and, in the case of a man, to the exclusion of his children, married people customarily have no community of goods. Bonds between siblings of the same mother are reported to be particularly strong to the extent that they think of one another's possessions as joint property. 'Borrowing between siblings cannot create debts and, as we know, a sibling is a person's first heir' (Fortes, 1950: 274).

These contrasting ties between spouses, fathers and their offspring, and matrikin are significant for the detailed analysis of production relations described in Chapters 4 and 5. Of particular importance is the distinction between the bond between fathers and their children, and a man and his sister's son.

In much of the literature, it is the affective ties between fathers and their offspring, particularly their sons, that are emphasised, together with the father's responsibility for providing their food and clothing and giving them a trade or education, thereby equipping them for the future. Nevertheless the same constraints on economic co-operation exist between fathers and sons as between spouses. Hence Schneider (1961) observes that economic co-operation between fathers and children, especially sons, is a serious threat to the solidarity of matrilineal descent groups.

Crucial for understanding the relation of a man and his sister's son is the latter's status as the former's potential heir. Thus the enmity between the two is emphasised while at the same time they are recognised as having common interests. As Fortes observes: 'No social relationship in Ashanti is so ambivalent' (Fortes, 1950: 272). Likewise, although bonds between siblings of the same mother are strong, there is the same ambiguity in the relationship, arising from their position as first heirs.

COCOA FARMING IN GHANA

The history of the development of cocoa production in Ghana has been covered extensively by Hill (1963). An important feature from the point of view of this study is that the initiative for the development and spread of the industry was largely indigenous and farmer oriented. Thus the production, as distinct from the sale, of cocoa beans, was largely undirected until the spread of diseases and pests made government involvement inevitable. The Ghana cocoa farmer has therefore frequently been cited as exemplifying the view that man in Africa behaves rationally and responds to incentives in the same way as economic man of classical economic theory (see Schneider, 1974a: 224).

The major government policy since the 1940s has been to encourage reinvestment of profits in farms devastated or even partly devastated by swollen shoot through programmes generally referred to as 'rehabilitation'. However, throughout the whole history of cocoa production, farmers have indeed reinvested their profits in cocoa, but in the continuous development of new farms on new lands, even using replanting grants for the development of totally new farms. In response, the government itself began to replace diseased trees, thereby avoiding cash compensation to offset replanting costs. The extent of government involvement is demonstrated most dramatically by the Eastern and Ashanti Region Rehabilitation Projects where farmer responsibility has been reduced in fact, but not in policy, to the signing of an agreement to place land within the development schemes (Adegboye and Okali, 1975). Apart from these schemes that have focused on farmers with already bearing farms there have been few attempts to provide credit directly to encourage farm expansion. The main source of capital for production has been through the farmers themselves.

Since there has been little replanting of trees, but rather the continuous establishment of new trees, the land under cocoa has increased until it covered, in 1970, 3.6 million acres representing 56 per cent of the cultivated area of the whole of Ghana and 70 per cent of that in southern Ghana (Ghana, Ministry of Agriculture, 1972). Much of this area coincides with that inhabited by the Akan (see Map 2.1). The industry has spread westward, with the oldest tree stock located in the Eastern Region and Eastern Ashanti and parts of the Volta Region, and the younger trees being located in the Brong Ahafo and Western Regions. The conditions under which farmers are operating today have therefore changed from those existing in the late nineteenth and early twentieth centuries, particularly with respect to land. Comparatively, farmers are operating in a land scarcity situation and they are travelling to more inaccessible places to acquire new land. In the old cocoa areas, for instance in Ashanti, uncultivated land is still available for cropping, but this is most likely to be reserved for producing food crops since mixed stands of cocoa and food can only be grown while the cocoa is young. Once the tree canopy has formed, except for small quantities of yam, food crops must be grown in separate stands and few cocoa farmers specialise in growing cocoa alone (Okali, Gyekye and Mabey, 1975). An investigation of the cocoa economy from the point of view of the farmer necessarily includes, therefore, his production of food crops that are invariably grown - if only for subsistence purposes - and compete for his factors of production including time and money.

Land for the establishment of cocoa has been acquired in various ways throughout the cocoa areas. Hill (1963) describes in detail the purchase of land in Akim Abuakwa during the late nineteenth and early twentieth centuries. Benneh (1970) and Adomako-Sarfoh (1965) have written of the acquisition of usufructuary rights in land under the jurisdiction of the Kumasi stools and ultimately the Asantehene. Beckett (1947) provides an early record of the acquisition of cultivation rights by stool subjects and strangers who were planting cocoa in the Eastern Region. He also covers the acquisition of planted farms as a result of indebtedness. Cases of hired

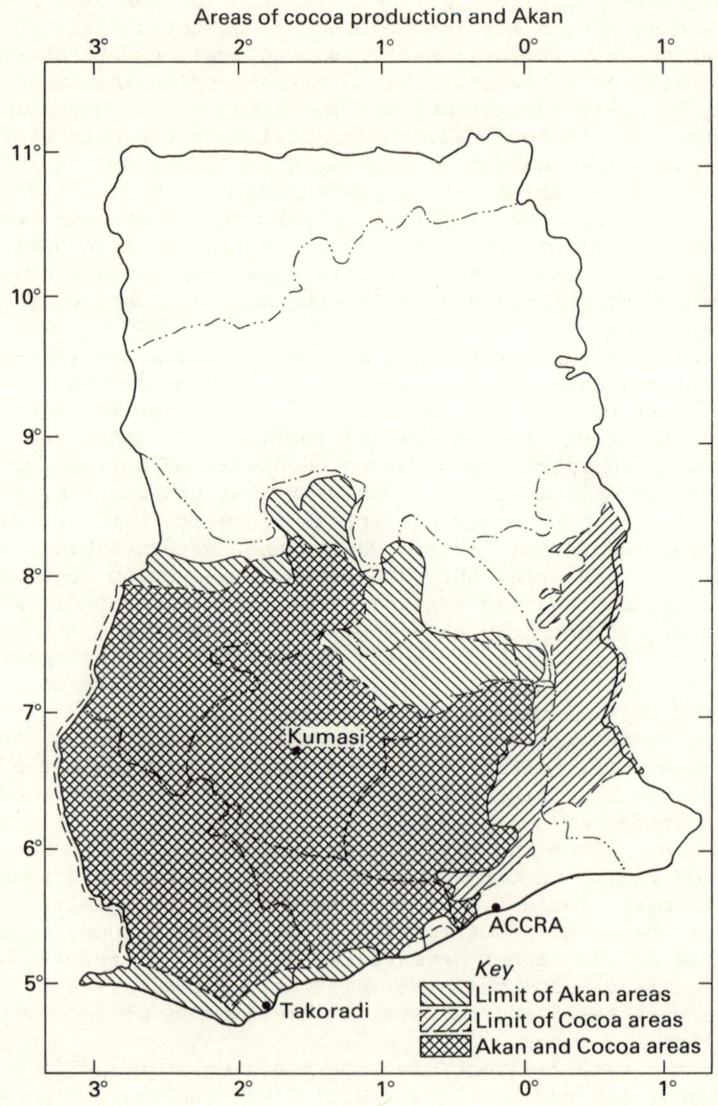
Areas of cocoa production and Akan
3°
2°
1°
0°
1°
11°
10°
9°
8°
7°
6°
5°
Kumasi
ACCRA
Takoradi
Key
Limit of Akan areas
Limit of Cocoa areas
Akan and Cocoa areas

Map 2.1

labourers acquiring parts of farms in payment for their management have been recorded as a well-established pattern in Buem areas of the Volta Region (Kotey, 1972).

The spread of the cocoa industry has therefore been based, not only on the increasing involvement of more persons in production, but also on the actual expansion of existing holdings from old to new areas. Thus holdings generally consist of a number of separate farms and Addo (1974) estimates that each farm owner has on average two. Descriptions of cocoa farmers have focused largely on those who have acquired farms outside their home areas, although by 1970 it was estimated that only 12 per cent of cocoa farm owners had their farms dispersed in more than one region (Ghana, Ministry of Agriculture, 1972).

Little detailed empirical information exists about the total population of cocoa farm owners. Addo's survey, completed in 1970 and based on a national sample taken from records of a single cocoa buying agency, provides demographic data (Addo, 1972 and 1974). Out of almost 4,000 farmers interviewed, the ratio of males to females was 9:1, males averaging fifty-four and females fifty-seven years of age. Hired workers were among the younger members of the agricultural labour force. Few farmers had received any formal education and just over one-third of his sample held a second occupation other than farming. In the pioneer cocoa areas, males were found to comprise a larger proportion of the farm population and farmers actually resident in the pioneer areas appear on the average to be younger than their counterparts elsewhere (Rourke, 1971).

The distribution of cocoa acreage and output among the population is highly skewed. The most recent information is given in the 1970 census of agriculture (Ghana, Ministry of Agriculture, 1972). On average, each holder was found to have 12 acres, with farmers from the Ashanti Region having the largest acreage, 22, while those from the Volta Region had the smallest, 5. Beckman (1970), focusing on differences in production rather than acreage, and using 1963 purchasing records of the monopsonistic United Ghana Farmers' Co-operative Council, calculated that 5 per cent of the cocoa farmers in that year sold over 12,000 lb of cocoa, accounting for 31 per cent of total sales. Addo (1974), on the other hand, estimates that up to 18 per cent produce this amount, while 40 per cent produce less than 3,000 lb.

The labour force engaged in cocoa production is large and varied, including both hired workers and relatives who may or may not be working for an agreed cash return. Thus Addo (1972), using the 1960 population census of Ghana, estimates that 32 per cent of the male and 25 per cent of the female members of the agricultural labour force were working, at least part of their time, in cocoa. Rourke (1971) details the various types of contract under which hired labourers work, including annual and piece-work contracts for cash, and other methods of payment based on production. Addo (1974) points out that almost all farmers have at some time hired temporary labourers to work on their farms while 60 per cent employed persons on long-term contracts.

The type of labour contracts used vary with the maturity of the farm. Annual contracts are reserved almost entirely for labourers working on young farms, whereas contracts involving payment by crop produced are obviously associated with mature farms. The most widely used among the latter are those where workers are paid by a percentage of crop produced, either one-third or half the production. Under this system, a farm owner leaves the tending of the farm to a person known as a caretaker who is responsible for completing all the farm work, while inputs for spraying with insecticides and accommodation are usually provided by the owner. Of all the contracts, labourers consider this to be the most advantageous and it is only under this arrangement that relatives are contracted. Relatives may include offspring caretaking for their father, a sister's son for his mother's brother, and descent group members for the corporate land-owning unit. All these arrangements are subject to tension and strain and frequently lead to open conflict, as demonstrated by the court records.

Besides hired labour, and relatives working as caretakers, farm owners also rely on relatives who work in various capacities, usually for no fixed return. Their role may be that of a supervisor, advising the often absent owner of requirements, or that of a manager, hiring labour and purchasing inputs and frequently themselves also providing labour. Finally, as in the majority of cases, they work merely as assistants, neither giving advice nor taking decisions, and usually therefore working side by side with the owner or representative acting as caretaker, supervisor or manager.

Land and labour are the most important production factors with which the cocoa farmers have to operate, since little equipment is necessary. The most common costly single item of equipment is a spraying machine and in some areas farmers prefer to hire persons to spray rather than attempt to purchase and maintain a machine themselves. The more common tools used are the cutlass and pruner, hoe and axe which, although they are subject to temporary scarcity, are comparatively cheap and therefore generally more accessible. Other farm inputs include the cocoa plant itself and shade plants which are used to protect the young cocoa trees. Plantain and cocoyam are used as the shade plants while at the same time in terms of their market value they are also the most important food items on the young farms. Cassava and vegetables may also be planted, while at least one corn harvest is taken during the first year. There is a premium on hybrid cocoa varieties owing to the reported high potential yield. The seeds are, however, notoriously scarce and reach only a small proportion of farmers.

Observable differences between farmers in the use of technological knowledge are small. Government planting programmes use a technology involving hybrid seedlings, line planting, wide spacing and interplanting with cocoyam and plantain (GCMB, n.d.). Although it is government policy to encourage all cocoa farmers to use such methods, farmers are less likely to have access to hybrid seedlings and are more likely to plant beans haphazardly and close together. They also do not restrict food crop planting to cocoyam and plantain. In spite of this apparent uniformity, some farmers are, as noted already, more successful in terms of cocoa output than others, and acquire more acres than others.

The cycle of activities on farms varies within the year and over the life of the tree. New farms are started between January and February with the felling of trees and land clearing, which includes the burning of the felled trees and other debris (Okali, 1975: 52-5). Frequently corn is planted and harvested first, followed by plantain, cocoyam and other food items, including vegetables. The cocoa itself follows. Weeding is already in progress before these activities are finished. Work from the end of the first year until the trees are almost fully mature is less varied. Food crops are harvested and the young trees sprayed, but the major time-consuming task is weeding; this reaches a peak between June and August. When new cocoa varieties are used, trees may start to bear fruit in the third year after planting. After this time, food items are reduced to almost nil. Work on mature farms also begins with weeding around June, cocoa harvesting being the only major time-consuming activity. In some parts of the cocoa areas two distinct cocoa harvests are common: a minor season from May to June and a major season starting in September. Once a farmer has farms that have reached different stages of maturity, each competes for the resources available. Work on mature farms is the most seasonal, being concentrated in the second half of the year, and dovetails with that on new farms which is most demanding in the first months. Peak work-loads occur in June, July and August when all farms require weeding.

DATA

The value of intensive studies of select samples of individuals, situations, groups or communities as a method of stimulating insights and for suggesting hypotheses for research has been demonstrated by Selltiz, Jahoda, Deutsch and Cook (1962). Basically it hinges on one central point, that as one turns to quantification the breadth of one's view must narrow as depth is substituted for it (Schneider, 1974a: 186).

In this study, therefore, a small number of farmers working in two cocoa farming communities are the main source of data for exploring the continuity of customs and correlates of change among cocoa farmers.

The choice of the two communities was determined firstly by the requirement that both should be basically Akan, one inhabited predominantly by citizens, the other by strangers. Secondly, it was essential that they should represent different stages in the life-cycle of farms and the farmers themselves. Akokoaso, an Akim village situated in the Eastern Region of Ghana, thirty miles east of Oda, was selected to represent an older cocoa farming community dominated by citizens (Map 2.2). Dominase, a farm camp situated fourteen miles north west of Mim, Ahafo, was the example chosen of a community where both farms and population were youthful.

The population at Akokoaso is aptly described, along with that of other villages, by Hill (1963) who observed that native Akims like those at Akokoaso, Asafo, Maase and Apapam would never move. Indeed, Hill's dramatisation of the migrant capitalist farmer was inspired by the myth of the sedentary peasant farmer which she suggests arose partly in consequence of the farming situation described by Beckett (1947) at Akokoaso.

Dominase was first settled in 1959 and in this respect is not

Location of survey sites in southern Ghana

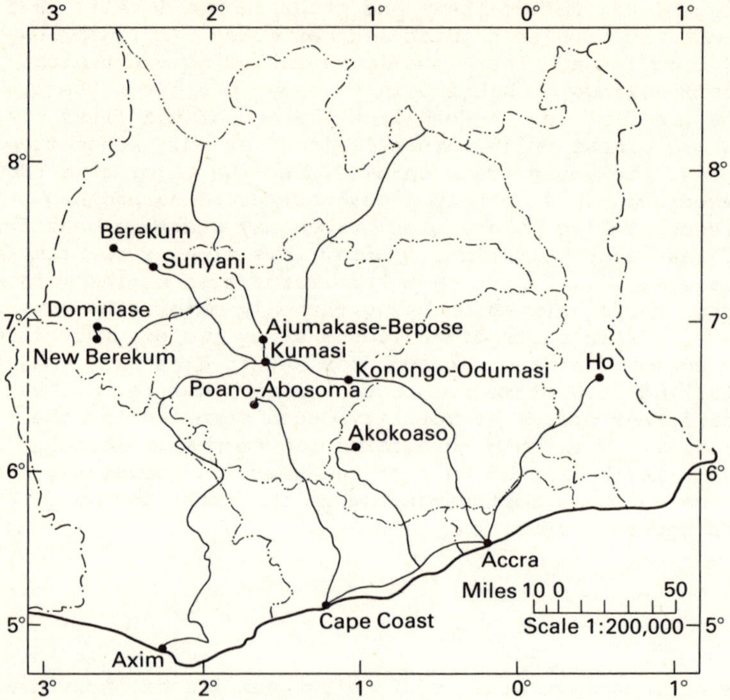

Map 2.2

atypical of Ahafo, where roughly 95 per cent of the villages recorded independently in the 1960 population census had been settled in the previous twelve-year period. Dominase itself was not independently recorded in 1960. Although by 1971, when the farm management study began, much of the immediate surrounding land had been allocated for cultivation, it was still a comparatively youthful settlement and new farms were being started annually.

Neither community is entirely Akan, and each contains both citizens and strangers. This is typical of communities in Ghana today, few of which remain entirely homogeneous with respect to citizenship or ethnicity. The presence of citizens and strangers in both, albeit in varying proportions, allowed important comparisons of citizens and strangers over space. Thus they fulfilled the requirements of the model and seemed suitable for providing comparative data that could be examined through in-depth studies of individuals.

Residence patterns, the distribution of farm ownership among the population and the structure of production units from these two communities are used to introduce the theme of changing production relations through space and over the life-cycle. These data were collected by means of a schedule while at the same time the interview was kept as open as possible to facilitate the detailing of other relevant information (Appendix 1). In this way individual reports of how farmers acquired their lands for cocoa were accumulated.

Farm management data and time budgets of members of production units cover a period of twelve months for a select group of fifteen Akan farmers who were working on the land surrounding Dominase, thus focusing on farmers working in mobile settings (Appendix 2). As is clearly indicated in Chapter 4, the fifteen farmers vary considerably in their pattern of farm development and their holdings range widely in both size and maturity. By combining their case histories and farm management data, it was therefore possible to view the various issues from a broad perspective before moving to a body of less detailed material. Comparative data for Akokoaso are provided through individual reports of how cocoa farms were acquired and from secondary sources.

Disputes brought before the civil courts of Ghana are used to illustrate problems arising from particular types of production relations. They are used as Turner (1957) uses his more detailed social dramas, to reflect different aspects of structural conflict. In justifying his technique, Turner points out that although the form and intensity of the dispute may be influenced by personality, it does not abolish the situation in which the conflict must arise. The analysis is restricted to cases covering land developed into cocoa farms involving people from matrilineal communities.

Discussions held with the chief at Mim, Ahafo, suggested that the majority of conflicts between relatives over land are settled in the traditional courts, or never appear in court because families consider it a disgrace to bring disagreements into public. No doubt time and money also limit the number of people who might be able to carry a dispute this far. It is not being suggested therefore that the issues observed from this analysis are the only ones arising from multiple interests in farms. However, such conflicts obviously have to be very important to reach the public courts.

The relevance of the court cases for this study lies less in the final judgments than in the arguments that the parties themselves present, since they are being used to demonstrate how people see their own situations, and the basis for their demands and expectations. Hence, once a case was filed in the courts it was included in the analysis even though it might have been discontinued for various reasons. This approach contrasts with the usual use of court records to emphasise the institutionalisation of changing rights of parties as decided by the courts (see Woodman, 1966, for instance).

Work was started at the courts where disputes over land at and around Dominase would appear. District Courts cover cases involving land valued up to ₵400.00; Circuit Courts handle land valued from ₵400.00 to ₵4,000.00; cases where property involved is in excess of this value, and estate cases, appear before the High Courts. Hence the District Court at Goaso, the Sunyani Circuit and High Courts were the first to be included. The High Courts located at Accra, Koforidua and Kumasi, the Circuit Courts at Koforidua and Kumasi and the District Court Grade I at Koforidua, were also covered for comparative purposes.

Where records permitted, all the cases involving cocoa properties that had appeared at the courts over the 1963-73 period were systematically examined and those involving related persons extracted. A number of files contained incomplete information, often because the parties failed to appear, or because an out of court settlement was reached, and the number of files actually checked did not necessarily always therefore correspond with the number listed in the court record book as having been filed. Litigation is a lengthy process often involving a number of years and the same case may be brought before a number of different courts because, for instance, of a revaluation of the property involved, or because of an appeal made to a higher court. In total 122 cases brought before the civil courts were found to be relevant (Appendix 3).

Finally, information was collected by single interviews with a number of farmers co-operating in government-directed planting and cocoa rehabilitation schemes in Ashanti, and this is used to examine the relevance of some of the findings to a different population of farmers (Appendix 4). The sample includes farmers from Beposo who were chosen to take part in a scheme organised by the Department of Co-operatives, and farmers co-operating in two Block Planting Schemes located at Abosoma and Odumasi, which at the time were in the hands of the Production Department of the Cocoa Marketing Board. Beposo was selected on the basis of the financial stability of the Co-operative Buying Association for that locality. The actual choice of farms was based on a technical assessment by the organisations concerned. Farms included in the schemes were those technically considered to be in need of better maintenance or, in the case of the Block Planting areas, that could be replanted. Thus the scheme did not necessarily include the total holding of the farmers concerned. This therefore seemed a suitable population for building up case histories of farm development using survey techniques and, in addition, for providing supporting information for some of the findings of the more detailed work. Although an attempt was made to interview all persons co-operating in these schemes, the number of interviews was finally limited by the mobility of the farmers involved. Some were working on cocoa farms located in other regions while others were engaged in non-farm occupations and living outside the locality.

CONCEPTUAL FRAMEWORK

In this analysis of cocoa farming, a major aim is to explain two aspects of production: the contribution made to farm development by offspring, parents, spouses and members of descent groups, and the distribution of returns. A framework needs to permit a meaningful analysis of the behaviour of the actors concerned - who include owners as individuals or corporate groups, supervisors, managers and assistants - and to distinguish between the various types of relationships existing between farm owners and co-workers. A particularly useful tool within this context is provided by the concept of social exchange as discussed by Schneider (1974a) and Ekeh (1974). In this analysis, the view that all forms of human interaction can be seen as a form of exchange is held.

Beginning with the contributions to farm development, since it is the allocations of land, time and money of the various actors that are being analysed, these resources can be considered as exchange items used to satisfy needs and desires which may include non-material items such as status. Although contributions to farm development do not necessarily confer beneficial rights in the property concerned, persons who invest in farms do expect reciprocation, either directly to themselves, or to a third party, or their contributions may represent the fulfilment of obligations incurred from previous exchanges. This study therefore focuses on understanding the change process itself and the items involved.

Significant aspects of the exchanges considered - affecting individuals and corporate groups - are the directness of the transaction, the time lapses between reciprocation and uncertainty of reciprocation. There is obviously a basic difference between situations where the terms of exchange are laid down, as for instance in the case of individuals hired to provide labour for an agreed rate of return to be paid at a specific time, who may or may not be relatives, and others where the terms are not precisely defined. Cocoa farmers and their assistants are involved in both types of situation. Epstein (1967) observed that the amount of personal involvement with those employed to help in the production process varies inversely with the amount of cash paid, suggesting that part of the payment for this labour is in the form of involvement or obligation. Certainly once exchange is between relatives it is rarely a strictly utilitarian transaction. Thus these exchanges, like those of gifts among the Trobrianders, are not purely free and gratuitous presentations, nor of purely interested and utilitarian production and exchange; they are kinds of hybrids (Mauss, 1974: 70).

A starting point is provided by the concepts of 'restricted' and 'generalised' exchange discussed by Ekeh (1974) while evaluating the contribution of Levi-Strauss to social exchange theory. Ekeh describes restricted exchange as a two-party transaction based on the principal of 'mutual reciprocity', in which each party expects to benefit the other directly. In contrast generalised exchange refers to actors benefiting others for which they do not expect direct or immediate reciprocation, and operates on the principle of 'univocal reciprocity' (Ekeh, 1974: 208). In this latter situation, no party gives to the person from whom he receives, and hence, as Ekeh himself points out, univocal reciprocity can only operate in an atmosphere of generalised morality and trust that the system will work.

Ekeh subdivides these basic types, and two subdivisions can be used to describe some of the exchanges in which the cocoa farmers are involved. Firstly he defines as 'exclusive restricted exchange' the situation where the dyadic relationship is totally isolated: $A \leftrightarrow B$; and secondly he defines as 'chain generalised exchange' the situation where the actors benefit others without expecting exchange: $A \rightarrow B \rightarrow C \rightarrow Z \rightarrow A$ (Ekeh, 1974: 209). There still remains the situation where the descent group may hire an individual, who may be a member, to work on corporate property. Since the exchange is direct, it belongs to the first category of exchanges, but is distinctly different in that it is more difficult to identify the actual parties involved. Within the same category lie the contractual relations between unrelated hired workers for whom the relationship terminates once payment has been made.

Arising from these two types of exchanges are relationships with varying degrees of stability. In restricted exchange, the actors can see clearly what is being gained and consequently it is a comparatively unstable relationship that can easily be terminated. The contractual relationship where amounts and timing are specified is the most brittle. Nevertheless, since in the case of cocoa farmers it may involve persons with whom one has affective and other ties, where the exchange transaction is not fulfilled, it may not lead to a break in the relationship altogether. Similarly, cocoa farmers are also involved in exchanges that are not necessarily immediately satisfied, and the terms are not clearly stated, even though reciprocation is direct. The more each party invests, the longer they may be prepared to wait for returns that may involve different items over time. Bearing this in mind, the relationship appears less unstable than Ekeh, for instance, suggests, since it can only survive, like generalised exchange, in an atmosphere of trust between the parties involved in which effective sanctions can be maintained.

As the relative status between actors involved in exchange situations changes, so also do their expectations. For instance the relative status of a young wife to her husband differs from that of a wife with adult children. When it is assumed therefore that actors may be operating on the basis of receiving returns in the future rather than the present, these returns will be based on expected future status with its associated rights and obligations. It is not possible to understand the basis of decision-making without introducing this time element and taking into account changes in the development cycle of the domestic group.

Finally there is the problem raised by Schneider (1974a) of the implications of satisfying the exchange equation. He is particularly concerned with the use of a medium of exchange, such as money, in the exchange transactions, and suggests that the payment for a good with a medium of exchange satisfies the exchange equation in a way that does not involve any continuing relationship between the parties. Among cocoa farmers, the media of exchange used include cash, land and developed farms in transactions involving relatives. Rather than assuming that their use precludes any continuing relationship, it is more appropriate to assume that the payment for a good with a medium of exchange may solve that particular contractual relationship, but it may also be followed by another contract, or place the relationship on an entirely different basis. Thus as with the gifts and presentations analysed by Mauss (1974), recipients are placed under an obligation that expresses subordination to the giver. Social exchanges can however offset each other, in which case an alliance is created that is manifested by expressions of respect and friendliness between the parties involved.

Using this frame for the analysis of the behaviour of cocoa farmers has implications for the study of social change itself. As Barth (1967) demonstrates, assuming a universal desire on behalf of people to reach an optimal allocation of time and money, the allocations may not be the same in all situations, but it is not necessary to assume that there have been changes in over-all values. Similarly, since profits in the view of the social exchange theorists include both social returns involving status and power, and economic returns involving cash, which itself can again be exchanged for a variety of goods including status and power, it is even possible to see new sources of material wealth sustaining customary means of acquiring power, for instance, if not for sustaining the same categories of people in power. Thus Schneider (1974b) writes of cocoa producers playing off one social exchange system against another, using something from one system to enhance status, and then translating it into their own system for profit. This view appears to place systems side by side which derives from Schneider's overall concern with how subsistence producers can become involved in the modern market economy without detriment to existing social values, and contrasts with the view that the allocations and exchanges underpin the structure of cocoa farming itself.

Chapter 3

Two cocoa farming communities

Akokoaso and Dominase both lie within the semi-deciduous rain forest belt that covers almost 80 per cent of the forest zone of Ghana. This belt is largely characterised by gently undulating topography, becoming more steep towards the east across the Volta River. The most representative soil groups in the belt are Forest Ochrosols and Rubrisols. These are red-yellow and yellow-brown upland soils which are highly suitable for tree crops like cocoa and coffee and for a wide variety of food crops.

The seasonality of rainfall determines to a large extent the cropping periods in the year. Annual rainfall ranges between 45 and 65 inches and follows a two-peak pattern. The principal rainy season extends from March to July with a maximum in June. The second rains fall between September and November with a maximum in October. Temperatures are uniformly high throughout the year and vary little from year to year, while the relative humidity varies between 70 to 80 per cent.

Although the two sites are essentially similar in climate, vegetation and soils, they vary considerably in length of settlement and hence in the period over which the land has been cultivated.

THE AKOKOASO COMMUNITY (1)

Akokoaso is an Akim village first settled in the late nineteenth century. The old part of the village is divided into wards occupied by the majority of the members of a single lineage and in this respect corresponds with the description by Fortes (1950) of a relatively stable community in Ashanti. Persons of non-Akan origin settled in the 1930s on the outskirts of the main village site and over the years this has become the area where the village has expanded. In 1933 there were 160 compounds of which 153 were occupied; by 1970 there were 270.

---

1 Information for 1933 is taken from Beckett (1947). Details of cocoa production and farming activities in 1970 are taken from Okali and Kotey (1971). Population data for 1930, 1960 and 1970 are taken from Ghana population census sources.

Beckett (1947) attributes the settlement of the people at Akokoaso to the internecine warfare between the Ashanti and Akims and internal migration arising out of the expansion of cocoa production. Although therefore he describes it as a relatively stable community, the Akan themselves had extensive ties with other areas of the country, particularly Ashanti, and these links are still retained today. However, in 1970, approximately two-thirds of the total population was born at Akokoaso itself.

Changes have occurred over time in the age-sex distribution of the population. In general the trend has been towards an increase in the proportion of persons aged under fifteen and over forty-four, with a complementary decrease in the working population between the ages of fifteen and forty-four until, in 1970, only 34 per cent of the population fell within this age group. Since 1960, the population has been dominated by females.

In the 1930s the majority of the working population were engaged in farming, even if they held another occupation, and cocoa was the major source of farm income. The first cocoa farms were established around 1900 and therefore by 1932 when Beckett's survey was started, a large part of the cocoa acreage had not reached maturity and almost 40 per cent of the farmers had only young farms on which food crops were still being grown. By 1970 this position had changed radically. Only 72 per cent of the employed population was engaged in agriculture compared with 88 per cent in 1933 and well over half of these were females, whereas in 1933 men dominated the agricultural scene. Although cocoa farming was still considered to be an important feature of farming activities in 1970, most cocoa was fifteen years old or more. New cocoa farms were less widely distributed and hence separate food production had increased. Production reached its peak in the 1964/5 crop year but had dropped to almost half the 1932/3 crop by 1969/70. Pressure on land was reported by farmers to be a major factor in the decline in production, reflecting a combination of inadequate acreage, poor soil and sites, and family and clan rights.

In the 1930s, since cocoa farms were young, most were still being operated by first owners; only 15 per cent of cocoa farm owners had any inherited farms. Citizens had free access to stool lands for farming without the necessity of obtaining permission from the chief, with, however, the restriction of family rights. Strangers acquired use rights from the chief.

Cocoa farm owners included both men and women; of the 267 independent cocoa farmers in 1933, 39 per cent were women. Information from cocoa buyers for the 1969/70 crop year suggests that female participation has declined to one-third of the total. This implication may be spurious, firstly because only persons with bearing cocoa were included, and secondly because producers of small crops frequently combined their produce with that of others for sale.

Differences in the size distribution of farms and incomes were recorded both in 1933 and 1970 and appear to have become more skewed over time. Over 80 per cent of the persons recorded making sales in 1969 sold less than twenty loads of cocoa, which comprised 12 per cent of total production, compared with 61 per cent of the sellers producing 21 per cent of total production in 1933/4.

THE DOMINASE COMMUNITY (2)

Dominase stands in complete contrast to Akokoaso, being a small community settled first in 1959, with only forty-two residential compounds in May 1972, at which time only the chief's house, a drinking bar and cocoa buying sheds were concreted. Like the whole of Ahafo District within which Dominase lies, the basis for settlement was laid by the timber companies, the largest of which, Mim timbers, started operations in this area in 1948 and began construction of the Bediakrom road to and beyond Dominase in 1954. The site was settled first by the present headman while he was a timber contractor and he established the first cocoa farms in the late 1950s.

In order for strangers to the Mim stool to farm in the area, permission must first be sought from the Mim chief who acts as caretaker of the lands on behalf of the Kumasi stool, under whose final jurisdiction the land lies. The relationship between the resident caretakers of land and the Kumasi stools and the resultant distinctive features of Ahafo landholding are described in detail by Arhin (1970) and Robertson (1973).

The Ahafo lands, including those covered in this survey, were presented by Nana Opoku Ware I to the occupants of the various stools in Kumasi after the Oborimoro war as their reward for defeating the enemy. The Ahafo lands are therefore under the jurisdiction of these Kumasi stools and the various adikrofo - headmen - living on the lands are the caretakers on their behalf.

Once permission to farm has been granted, the agreement is sealed by the offer of a 'drink' comprising both cash and drinks by the stranger farmer. In addition to the first payment of 'drink' made to acquire cultivation rights, a further annual rent is levied when the trees are mature. In the case of the survey sites, this rent should go to the Ministry of Lands and Mineral Resources at Goaso. Benneh (1970) has described a system of tribute as it occurs in Sefwi Wiawso, another pioneer cocoa area, whereby a tenant pays one-tenth of the proceeds realised from the sale of his cocoa on mature farms but also pays a fixed rent on non-bearing farms. The proceeds are divided between the central government, the local council and the traditional rulers who, as reported by Arhin (1970), are greater in number than in Ashanti and include the Asantehene, the respective Kumasi clan chiefs, the landholding Kumasi clan chiefs and the adikrofo as administrators and caretakers.

The timber activities and suitable forest for cocoa farming have attracted both a migrant and a working population. Hence in 1970, only one in twelve persons there had been born at Dominase itself; the majority had emigrated from another region of Ghana, particularly the men. The women appear to have emigrated from less distant places. In 1970 just over 60 per cent of the population was over fifteen years of age and among these, only 6 per cent were over forty-four years of age. Younger persons formed a comparatively small proportion of the population, particularly those in the age group ten to fourteen, most of whom were living elsewhere while

---

2 Background information is taken from Okali (1975), census data for 1970 from Ghana population census sources.

attending school. Dominase was still regarded as a farm camp site even though it was far from the home towns of many of the residents. The majority of the population therefore regarded their stay as temporary and although a primary school was established there in 1971, a large number of people sent their children home to primary school.

In contrast to Akokoaso, almost two-thirds of all residents at Dominase in 1970 were male and hence almost two in every three members of the agricultural labour force were also male. The majority of the working population was employed full or part time in farming and cocoa was the major crop produced. Since a large proportion of the cocoa farms were still young, food crops were an important source of income from them and were the main source of food for consumption. In general, once payment for cultivation rights had been made, farmers were unwilling to use such land solely for the cultivation of food crops. Farmers wishing to plant food in addition to that grown on the cocoa farms would do so in their home towns and reserve it there for home use.

RESIDENCE PATTERNS

Differences in the settlement pattern between Akokoaso and Dominase are reflected in the residential arrangements from which related factors can be deduced. Later, the various residential forms are examined in relation to production arrangements. With whom people live is obviously determined by the range of choice available, and a distinction is made between broad categories of individuals who might be expected to differ significantly in their residence patterns. The stranger and the unmarried, including those who have never married, the widowed and divorced, each have a narrower range of relatives with whom they might choose to live than the citizen and the married person.

Compounds are described firstly by reference to the age and sex of the head. The head was determined by the compound members themselves and there is no assumed relationship between the position of the head and a particular role performance. Fortes (1950) demonstrates that domestic groups under a male head characterise a parental family that may include the head's sister and her children and the children of his children or of his nieces.

As the ultimate focus of this analysis is work units, data are restricted to persons of fifteen years and above who were not in school and, when referring to all compound members as distinct from heads, only to those working within agriculture. A person's residence is defined according to the compound in which he or she eats; thus a residence unit refers to a collectivity of people eating under the same roof. Compound members may therefore subdivide for various activities, and form almost totally distinct units, being related only as landlords and tenants.

Information on residence and production arrangements was collected from 104 compounds at Akokoaso in 1973 (Table 3.1). All compounds in the more recently settled part of the village were included, whereas long-established compounds in the village centre, where mostly citizens reside, were underrepresented, mainly because of the difficulty of locating all members at a single place at any one time and the unwillingness of people to give information about absent members.

TABLE 3.1 Labour force in 104 compounds at Akokoaso in 1973

Farmer, fifteen+	Citizens[a]	Strangers	Total
Male	59	28	87
Female	118	23	141
Non-farmer, fifteen+			
Male	25	33	58
Female	22	11	33
Total	224	95	319

[a]For a definition of citizenship see p. 13.

Membership of compounds ranged from one to sixteen adults, averaging three. The largest compound included a landlord and tenants while the smallest was usually inhabited only by a woman. Just over half the residents were women who, as recorded in the 1970 census, were more likely than their male counterparts to be working within agriculture. Although a third of the residents were strangers, 80 per cent of the compounds were headed by stool citizens. Over half the citizen heads were female, reflecting their representation in the population. Among stranger heads males dominated and two out of three of the stranger population were men (Table 3.2).

TABLE 3.2 Compound heads by citizenship and marital status at Akokoaso

	Male compound heads		Female compound heads	
	Citizens %	Strangers %	Citizens %	Strangers %
Married				
Citizen spouse	58.8	25.0	28.0	25.0
Stranger spouse	17.7	56.2	24.0	25.0
Citizen and stranger spouse	8.8	6.3	-	-
Not married	14.7	12.5	48.0	50.0
Total	100.0	100.0	100.0	100.0
Number of compounds	34	16	50	4

Male and female heads differed distinctly in their age, marital and occupational status. Women in the position of heads of domestic units were younger and less likely to be currently married than their male counterparts. Only five heads were recorded as having no occupation, all of whom were women over sixty years of age who considered themselves retired. Four others were working outside agriculture, a woman who was trading and three men including a timber contractor, palm wine tapper and driver.

Intermarriage between citizens and strangers is a fairly common occurrence at Akokoaso, and even among compound heads 25 per cent had formed such unions.

Residence units fell into two main types:

1 those grouped around husbands and wives, and
2 those grouped around an effective minimal lineage or part of it, including a woman and her sisters or daughters, or a man and his sisters or sister's son (Table 3.3).

In addition there were a few men living with their offspring or jointly with their wives, siblings or affines.

TABLE 3.3 Types of compound at Akokoaso

Adult compound members	Compound heads Males %	Females %	All %
Spouse ± offspring ± grandchildren	54.0	22.2	37.5
± offspring ± grandchildren	14.0	61.1	38.4
Siblings and/or sister's children	20.0	16.7	18.3
Spouse + siblings/ affines	6.0	-	2.9
Others[a]	6.0	-	2.9
Total	100.0	100.0	100.0
Number of compounds	50	54	104

[a] Three cases of men living with their deceased mother's brother's wife and children or father's heir.

The incidence of the two main types of residence varied according to the sex of the head of the residence unit. Male heads characterised a parental family unit, although a younger sister's children might also have been sharing the same residence. Men living with their adult dependants by matrilineal kinship formed the next most common arrangement. In contrast, co-residence of women and their dependants by parenthood dominated compounds with female heads, whereas less than one in four of these included a woman and her other dependants by matrilineal kinship. Overall, only a small proportion of compounds contained non-lineage kin living under the domestic jurisdiction of a female.

In order to examine effectively the balance between ties of marriage, parenthood and matrilineal kinship for determining types of residence unit, the marital status and citizenship of the head must be considered.

One in every three compound heads were not married, just over two two-thirds of whom were women. In the majority of residence units headed by unmarried women, adult membership was restricted almost entirely to their offspring and grandchildren rather than to other matrikin (Table 3.4). On the other hand, residence units grouped around unmarried male heads were more likely to comprise groups of siblings or were cases where a man had acquired his headship through inheritance.

It was only among residence units under male heads that domestic arrangements were grouped around persons related through kinship, marriage and affinity, and all these instances concerned strangers. Thus the composition of residence units headed by citizens and strangers differed, with those that were basically segments of matrilineages headed by citizens. Frequently, the only ties in a locality of stranger heads, who were mainly men, were through marriage and thus their residence units were usually grouped around themselves and their wives. One exception was a woman married to a citizen who lived elsewhere in the village while she herself rented a room in her compound to a tenant. Among the male stranger heads, three of the four who were married to citizens lived with them even when this involved also living with the wife's sisters. The other case involved a polygamous union, where the man lived with his stranger spouse while his citizen spouse lived in her own separate compound.

Residential arrangements, then, are also a function of type of marital alliance. Among strangers, as observed already, residence units were usually grouped around spouses. When the residence units headed by citizens were grouped around spouses, the spouse was frequently a stranger (Table 3.5). Among compounds headed by a woman, type of marital alliance was particularly important for determining whether or not she would be the head, since once a woman was married to a citizen and residing with him he was usually referred to as the head.

Of interest, therefore, were the three compounds grouped around husbands and wives but headed by female citizens married to citizens. The first involved a forty-one-year-old woman whose husband claimed that although he had his own house he preferred to live with his wife. The house in which they were living was built by her father. The second was a thirty-eight-year-old woman whose husband was a hunter; she gave no details as to how she acquired the house. The last, who at thirty-five was the youngest, reported that she had built the house herself.

Looking at the residence of all compound members, the distinct difference between citizens and strangers in the importance of marriage for determining residence is retained (Table 3.6). Thus almost three-quarters of both Akan and non-Akan strangers lived in the same residence units as their wives (Table 3.7). Again, where

TABLE 3.4 Types of compound at Akokoaso

Adult compound members	Compound heads: Citizens, Married, Male %	Citizens, Married, Female %	Citizens, Not married, Male %	Citizens, Not married, Female %	Citizens, All %	Strangers, Married, Male %	Strangers, Married, Female %	Strangers, Not married, Male %	Strangers, Not married, Female %	Strangers, All %
Spouse ± offspring ± grandchildren	55.2	42.3			32.1	78.6	50.0			60.0
Spouse + affines	-	-				21.4	-			15.0
Offspring ± grandchildren	13.8	50.0	20.0	70.8	41.7	-	50.0	100.0	100.0	25.0
Siblings and/or sister's children	24.1	7.7	60.0	29.2	22.6	-	-	-	-	-
Other[a]	6.9	-	20.0	-	3.6	-	-	-	-	-
Total	100.0	100.0	100.0	100.0	100.0	100.0	100.0	100.0	100.0	100.0
Number of compounds	29	26	5	24	84	14	2	2	2	20

[a] Three cases of men living with their deceased mother's brother's wife and children or father's heir.

Note: Male citizens were in all cases married to Akan women whereas female citizens were married to Akans and non-Akans.

TABLE 3.5 Types of compound at Akokoaso by marital alliance of citizen heads

Adult compound members	Citizen Spouse			Stranger spouse		
	Males %	Females %	All %	Males %	Females %	All %
Spouse ± offspring ± grandchildren	50.0	21.4	38.2	66.7	66.7	66.7
± Offspring ± grandchildren	20.0	64.3	38.2	-	33.3	19.0
Sibling and/or sister's children	25.0	14.3	20.6	22.2	-	9.5
Others[a]	5.0	-	3.0	11.1	-	4.8
Total	100.0	100.0	100.0	100.0	100.0	100.0
Number of married citizens	20	14	34	9	12	21

[a]Two cases of men living with their deceased mother's brother's wife and offspring.

Note: For men refers to those with at least one stranger spouse. He may also be married to a citizen.

TABLE 3.6 Residence of citizens and strangers at Akokoaso

Adult co-residents	Citizens				Strangers			
	Married		Not married		Married		Not married	
	Male %	Female %	Male %	Female %	Male %	Female %	Male %	Female %
Spouse ± offspring ± grandchildren	37.3	29.4			70.8	66.6		
Spouse + affines	-	4.7			12.5	19.0		
Offspring ± grandchildren	5.9	14.1	25.0	51.5	-	4.8	50.0	100.0
Mother, siblings + other matrikin	37.2	44.7	37.5	45.5	-	-	-	-
Father + siblings/ parents	11.8	7.1	12.5	-	4.2	4.8	-	-
Other	7.8[a]	-	25.0[a]	3.0[a]	8.3	4.8	-	-
Tenant	-	-	-	-	4.2	-	50.0	-
Total	100.0	100.0	100.0	100.0	100.0	100.0	100.0	100.0
Number of residents	51	85	8	33	24	21	4	2

[a] Heirs, wife and offspring of deceased.

Note: Includes only members of the agricultural labour force who were aged fifteen+.

TABLE 3.7 Residence of strangers at Akokoaso

Adult co-residents	Akan				Non-Akan			
	Married		Not married		Married		Not married	
	Male %	Female %	Female %	All %	Male %	Female %	Male %	All %
Spouse ± offspring ± grandchildren	66.7	71.6		64.0	73.2	57.1		57.7
Spouse + affines	22.2	7.1		12.0	6.7	42.9		15.5
Offspring ± grandchildren	-	7.1	100.0	12.0	-	-	50.0	7.7
Father + siblings/ parents	-	-	-	-	6.7	-	-	3.8
Other[a]	11.1	7.1	-	8.0	6.7	-		3.8
Tenant	-	7.1	-	4.0	6.7	-	50.0	11.5
Total	100.0	100.0	100.0	100.0	100.0	100.0	100.0	100.0
Number of residents	9	14	2	25	15	7	4	26

[a]One male co-residing with affines only and in the second instance the relationship is not clear. One female co-residing with grandfather.

Notes: Includes only members of the agricultural labour force who were aged fifteen+. Six of the male and nine of the female Akan were married to citizens. Ten non-Akan men had citizen spouses.

citizens were married to strangers, they were more likely to co-reside with them (Table 3.8). Nevertheless, men and women did differ in this respect. One in three of the female citizens were married to non-resident strangers compared with less than one in five of the men, and hence, unlike their male counterparts, they were more likely to be living with their matrikin. On the other hand all citizens married to citizens had similar residence patterns.

Men were more likely to be living with their fathers than women, whose closer ties with their mothers and their own offspring for residence purposes are demonstrated throughout. One instance stood out of a woman living with her husband in her mother's compound. Few details of the man were given except that his main occupation was hunting.

Finally, among the unmarried, who were principally women, ties of motherhood were important for determining residence.

The pattern of domestic residence at Dominase reflected that of the strangers at Akokoaso, since none of the Dominase residents were living in their home town although a number were citizens. Dominase was a highly mobile settlement and residents spent a considerable amount of time travelling to and from their home towns. Information was collected from thirty-eight of the forty-two residential compounds at Dominase in 1972; the remaining compounds were vacant at the time (Table 3.9). Compounds included between one and ten adult members, averaging three. As suggested by the 1970 population census of Ghana, males were more numerous than females, and only five persons were working totally outside the agricultural sector; one woman and four men. Although the 1970 population census of Ghana recorded 23 per cent of the resident women at Dominase as homemakers, this was not supported by the survey. Only women who had recently given birth were found to spend their whole time staying within the compound looking after their children, and after three months they would resume work on the farms.

Almost two-thirds of the residents in these compounds had lived at the site for less than six years and had emigrated from other parts of Ghana, particularly Brong Ahafo and Ashanti (Table 3.10). Male residents had emigrated from farther afield than their female counterparts, almost a third of whom were citizens.

Since Dominase is an immigrant settlement, the majority of compound heads were strangers and among these, as at Akokoaso, males predominated (Table 3.11). In contrast compounds headed by citizens were dominated by females. Again, as at Akokoaso, women in the position of compound heads were frequently not married and so, for them, there was no question of marital ties determining residence.

The most common residence unit was grouped around husbands and wives whether the heads were citizens or strangers (Table 3.12). Nevertheless, the composition of residence units headed by men and women differed. Thus all those headed by women, two-thirds of whom were citizens, contained their dependants by motherhood. Two of these instances involved married women: a citizen whose spouse was a timber worker living at another site, and a stranger whose spouse lived in a separate compound with his senior wife. In all other instances where husbands and wives were living at Dominase, they were co-resident.

TABLE 3.8 Residence of citizens by marital alliance at Akokoaso

Compound members	Citizen spouse			Stranger spouse		
	Males %	Females %	All %	Males %	Females %	All %
Spouse ± offspring	30.7	30.8	30.8	58.4	27.3	35.6
Spouse + affines	-	1.9	1.1	-	9.1	6.7
± Offspring ± grandchildren	7.7	11.5	9.9	-	18.2	13.3
Mother, siblings + other matrikin	38.5	46.2	42.8	33.3	42.4	40.0
Father + siblings/ parents	15.4	9.6	12.1	-	3.0	2.2
Other[a]	7.7	-	3.3	8.3	-	2.2
Total	100.0	100.0	100.0	100.0	100.0	100.0
Number of married citizens	39	52	91	12	33	45

[a] Two living with their father's heir and two with their deceased mother's brother's wife and children.

Note: Includes only members of the agricultural labour force who were aged fifteen+.

TABLE 3.9 Labour force in thirty-eight compounds at Dominase in 1972

Farmer, fifteen+	Citizens	Strangers	Total
Male	6	54	60
Female	14	33	47
Non-farmer, fifteen+			
Male	-	4	4
Female	-	1	1
Total	20	92	112

TABLE 3.10 Origin of Dominase residents aged fifteen and over

Region of origin	Males %	Females %	Total %
Brong Ahafo			
Stool citizens	9.4	29.2	17.9
Others	28.1	37.5	32.1
Ashanti	26.6	12.5	20.5
Central	-	2.1	0.9
Northern	18.7	8.3	14.3
Volta	17.2	10.4	14.3
Total	100.0	100.0	100.0
Number of persons	64	48	112

TABLE 3.11 Compound heads by citizenship and marital status at Dominase

	Male compound heads		Female compound heads	
	Citizens	Strangers	Citizens	Strangers
	%	%	%	%
Married				
Citizen spouse	75.0	14.3	20.0	-
Stranger spouse	25.0	78.6	-	100.0
Not married	-	7.1	80.0	-
Total	100.0	100.0	100.0	100.0
Number of compounds	4	28	5	1

TABLE 3.12 Types of compound at Dominase

Adult compound members	Citizen compound heads				Stranger compound heads			
	Married		Not married		Married		Not married	
	Male %	Female %	Female %	All %	Male %	Female %	Male %	All %
Spouse ± offspring	100.0	-	-	44.4	76.9	-	-	72.7
Spouse + others[a]	-	-	-	-	19.2	-	-	15.1
Offspring	-	100.0	100.0	55.6	-	100.0	50.0	6.1
Other[b]	-	-	-	-	3.9	-	50.0	6.1
Total	100.0	100.0	100.0	100.0	100.0	100.0	100.0	100.0
Number of compounds	4	1	4	9	26	1	2	29

[a] Four with siblings and one with in-laws.

[b] One with son and sister's son and one with sister's son only.

Although dwelling units were largely grouped around spouses, and over 90 per cent of married persons lived in the same compound as their spouses, almost one-third of the married adult residents were also living with other kin (Table 3.13). This pattern is similar for both Akan and non-Akan strangers (Table 3.14). Since most women were brought to Dominase by their husbands, it was their kinsmen that were usually co-resident. The only man co-residing with his affines was married to a citizen who prior to marriage was living at Dominase with her mother from Mim town and stepfather from a different town. Just over one-fifth of the population had relatives either living in another compound at Dominase or at a nearby site, but these were also more likely to be relatives of the men. Thus almost two-thirds of the women with other relatives nearby were stool citizens, but even they, as observed already, were living with their husbands.

In contrast to this pattern of living at Dominase, when immigrants return to their home town spouses do not commonly co-reside; both men and women normally live with their own kin.

The significant feature of the forms of residence units identified at both Akokoaso and Dominase was that women in the position of heads of domestic units were frequently not married - mostly either widowed or divorced - or were married to strangers. Since the majority of female strangers migrated with their husbands, rather than with their own kin, women heading compounds were more likely to be single and citizens.

The overall comparison between Akokoaso and Dominase emphasises the uniformity in residential arrangements in mobile settings, where the possibility of separating ties of descent, marriage and parenthood can no longer be maintained for residence purposes. The significance of mobility is emphasised further when residence units involving Akan strangers in the two communites are compared. Both men and women may co-reside with their affines, and thus live in situations that are customarily regarded as tension-filled and therefore precarious.

The question now being asked is in what way, if at all, these residence patterns are linked with economic arrangements.

PRODUCTION PATTERNS

Akokoaso and Dominase differ in their agricultural production patterns. Two features are particularly relevant, the first being the predominance of young cocoa farms at Dominase and the use of these for subsistence purposes, contrasting with the maturity of the cocoa farms at Akokoaso and the reliance on separate farms for food supplies. The second concerns the two populations, one dominated by women, the other by men.

The production patterns in the two settlements are compared firstly by looking at the distribution of farm ownership among the population and secondly by looking at the composition of production units. A production unit is defined as any individual or group of individuals engaged in or organised for the purpose of engaging in productive activity. Since citizenship and marital status have been identified as important variables determining headship and

TABLE 3.13 Residence of citizens and strangers at Dominase

Adult co-residents	Citizens					Strangers				
	Married		Not married			Married		Not married		
	Male %	Female %	Male %	Female %	All %	Male %	Female %	Male %	Female %	All %
Spouse ± offspring	100.0	70.0			55.0	63.2	68.8			52.9
Spouse + other	-	20.0			10.0	28.9	25.0			23.0
± Offspring	-	10.0	-	100.0	25.0	-	3.1	6.3	-	2.3
Siblings	-	-	-	-	-	2.6	-	18.7	-	4.6
Parents	-	-	100.0	-	10.0	-	-	18.7	100.0	4.6
Tenants	-	-	-	-	-	-	-	25.0	-	4.6
Others	-	-	-	-	-	5.3	3.1	31.3	-	8.0
Total	100.0	100.0	100.0	100.0	100.0	100.0	100.0	100.0	100.0	100.0
Number of residents	4	10	2	4	20	38	32	16	1	87

TABLE 3.14 Residence of strangers at Dominase

Adult co-residents	Akan					Non-Akan			
	Married		Not married			Married		Not married	
	Male %	Female %	Male %	Female %	All %	Male %	Female %	Male %	All %
Spouse ± offspring	57.7	73.9			55.2	66.7	55.6		48.3
Spouse + other	30.8	21.7			22.4	33.3	33.3		24.2
± Offspring	-	4.4	12.5	-	3.4	-	-	-	-
Siblings	3.8	-	-	-	1.8	-	-	37.5	10.3
Parents	-	-	37.5	100.0	6.9	-	-	-	-
Tenants	-	-	25.0	-	3.4	-	-	25.0	6.9
Others	7.7	-	25.0	-	6.9	-	11.1	37.5	10.3
Total	100.0	100.0	100.0	100.0	100.0	100.0	100.0	100.0	100.0
Number of residents	26	23	8	1	58	12	9	8	29

composition of dwelling units, they are also considered in this analysis, while account is taken too of the age structure of the farm population.

A large proportion of persons in the agricultural labour force at Akokoaso owned farms (Table 3.15). Although a distinction can be drawn between persons growing food and cocoa and those growing only food crops, most people when pressed admitted to having at least a little cocoa, although for many the amount of cocoa involved was small and not therefore the main source of income. Farm ownership was, however, mainly restricted to citizens and men, while both Akan and non-Akan strangers, and women, formed a large proportion of assistants on farms. Thus farm ownership was most restricted among female strangers.

Since strangers have no automatic rights to land at Akokoaso they comprised the hired labour force. A number had, however, acquired farming rights in various ways. Among the male strangers, including both Akans and non-Akans, who were farm owners, seven acquired land for cocoa through purchase or gift from the chief as a result of long residence. Two others claimed that they were planting for themselves on land acquired from their local wives. Among the female strangers, three Akans owned farms: one had acquired land for cocoa growing from her father, who was a citizen, a second acquired land from her husband, also a citizen. The third, having come to Akokoaso with her mother's brother and her own brother from Ashanti many years ago, was growing only food crops on land acquired through long residence. As can be seen from these cases, strangers do not form a distinct category of persons. A number had relatives from Akokoaso who had acquired land in various ways, although their own mothers were not of the town. Through these people and local spouses, they were able to acquire farming rights, although their rights were not always clearly defined. Nevertheless once people are allowed to grow cocoa, their rights appear to be tolerably secure.

Although female citizens did have rights to farm land, they were less likely to own farms than their male counterparts and a large proportion specialised in growing food crops. Among the men, only strangers who had limited rights to farm land were growing food crops only and for these, farming was a second occupation. Male citizens, therefore, once they were working within agriculture, were usually able to rise to farm ownership. However, the position occupied by people in the labour force changed during the course of their lives. As they aged, both men and women were more likely to own cocoa farms than assist on the farms of other people (Table 3.16). Women however were involved in food production from an early age and therefore began working as independent cultivators before men.

The relationship between marital status and position in the agricultural labour force varied (Table 3.17). Among male citizens, almost all unmarried persons were young and they assisted on farms rather than owned farms, whereas among strangers, married men frequently assisted others, which was consistent with their restricted cultivation rights. In contrast, among female citizens, who included a large number of older women no longer married, it was those who were not married who were more likely to have risen to farm

TABLE 3.15 The agricultural labour force at Akokoaso

	Males				Females			
	Citizens	Strangers		All	Citizens	Strangers		All
		Akan	Non-Akan			Akan	Non-Akan	
	%	%	%	%	%	%	%	%
Farm owners								
Cocoa and food	93.2	22.3	47.3	75.9	48.3	25.0	-	43.3
Food only	-	33.3	5.3	4.6	30.5	6.2	-	26.2
Assistants								
Assists relative	6.8	33.3	15.8	11.5	20.3	68.8	100.0	29.8
Hired worker	-	11.1	31.6	8.0	0.9	-	-	0.7
Total	100.0	100.0	100.0	100.0	100.0	100.0	100.0	100.0
Number of persons	59	9	19	87	118	16	7	141

TABLE 3.16 Farm ownership through life at Akokoaso

Farm owner	Males						Females					
	15-24 %	25-44 %	45-64 %	65+ %	NI %	Total %	15-24 %	25-44 %	45-64 %	65+ %	NI %	Total %
Cocoa and food	-	69.2	90.0	92.9	53.3	75.9	11.1	28.6	75.6	77.8	16.7	43.3
Food only	-	11.5	3.3	-	-	4.6	22.2	27.1	19.5	22.2	50.0	26.2
Assists relative	100.0	15.4	-	-	26.7	11.5	66.7	42.9	4.9	-	33.3	29.8
Hired worker	-	3.9	6.7	7.1	20.0	8.0	-	1.4	-	-	-	0.7
Total	100.0	100.0	100.0	100.0	100.0	100.0	100.0	100.0	100.0	100.0	100.0	100.0
Number of persons	2	26	30	14	15	87	9	70	41	9	12	141

NI: No information.

TABLE 3.17 Farm ownership by citizenship and marital status at Akokoaso

	Citizens				Strangers			
	Married		Not married		Married		Not married	
	Males %	Females %	Males %	Females %	Males %	Females %	Males %	Females %
Farm owners								
Cocoa and food	98.0	45.9	62.5	54.5	37.5	9.5	50.0	100.0
Food only	-	28.2	-	36.4	16.7	4.8	-	-
Assistants								
Assists relative	2.0	24.7	37.5	9.1	25.0	85.7	-	-
Hired worker	-	1.2	-	-	20.8	-	50.0	-
Total	100.0	100.0	100.0	100.0	100.0	100.0	100.0	100.0
Number of persons	51	85	8	33	24	21	4	2

ownership. Significantly, among the female strangers the only two single women were farm owners.

Excluding persons working as hired labourers, assistance was given mostly to spouses and secondly to parents (Table 3.18). Nevertheless, male citizens were working exclusively for parents, including one married man whose father claimed that the son had actually planted cocoa himself in addition to continuing to work for him. Among strangers, on the other hand, even men reported that they were assisting their spouses more than other people. Similarly, although married female citizens assisted their husbands, it was immigrant wives who were most likely to be found working on their husbands' farms. It is not clear, however, whether women were assisting on cocoa or food farms since the larger proportion of cocoa farms at Akokoaso were mature and generally in the hands of caretakers.

TABLE 3.18 Relationship of farm owners to assistants at Akokoaso

Relationship	Citizens				Strangers	
	Married		Not married		Married	
	Male %	Female %	Male %	Female %	Male %	Female %
Spouse	-	57.1			83.3	88.9
Mother	-	33.3	66.7	100.0	-	11.1[a]
Father	100.0	4.8	33.3	-	-	-
Mother's brother	-	4.8	-	-	-	-
Other	-	-	-	-	16.7[b]	-
Total	100.0	100.0	100.0	100.0	100.0	100.0
Number of assistants	1	21	3	3	6	18

[a] Parents.

[b] Relationship not clear.

Finally, among married citizens the incidence of farm ownership was greater among those married to strangers (Table 3.19). This difference according to marital alliance was particularly distinctive in the case of female citizens. One in three of those married to citizens were working as assistants compared with only one of those married to strangers. Although male strangers married to citizens did assist on their wives' farms, the advantageous position of these women with respect to cocoa farm ownership did not appear to be linked to any real difference in assistance that they might receive. Thus when farmers were asked to report on help that they were receiving on farms there was little difference in responses from women married to strangers and those married to citizens (Table 3.20). A number of these stranger spouses were in fact planting on their wives' land and such enterprises are unlikely to be joint concerns, or those of the husbands.

TABLE 3.19 Farm ownership among Akokoaso citizens by marital alliance

	Citizen spouse		Stranger spouse	
	Males %	Females %	Males %	Females %
Farm owner				
Cocoa and food	97.4	42.3	100.0	51.5
Food only	-	25.0	-	33.4
Assistants				
Assists spouse	-	21.2	-	3.0
Assists other relative	2.6	9.6	-	12.1
Hired worker	-	1.9	-	-
Total	100.0	100.0	100.0	100.0
Number of citizens	39	52	12	33

TABLE 3.20 Marital alliances of Akokoaso citizens and assistance received on cocoa farms

Assistants	Farm owners			
	Citizen spouse		Stranger spouse	
	Males %	Females %	Males[a] %	Females %
No one	57.5	54.6	50.0	64.7
Mother	-	9.1	-	-
Spouse	30.0	31.8	50.0	35.3
Offspring/ grandchildren	2.5	-	-	-
No reply	10.0	4.5	-	-
Total	100.0	100.0	100.0	100.0
Number of citizens	40	22	10	17

[a]A number had more than one wife, usually one a stranger.

One stranger whose wife was deceased did note that he was working on his daughter's farm which she had acquired from her mother. As observed already, no male citizens reported that they were working as assistants on their wives' farms; two, however, were planting on their wives' land and are described below:

> Ama Kwakwa, a citizen, is 41 years old and lives with her husband in a house built by her father. She has two cocoa plots. One, on which her husband also works, is a young farm planted on land which she acquired through her grandmother; a second, which is now in the hands of a hired caretaker, she acquired already planted from her father. Ama claims that this latter is her most important farm since it is the only one giving any income; the other is still young. Her 50-year-old husband, also a citizen, has his own land which he says he has neglected since he prefers to work on that of his wife, which is better. He also says that he has a house of his own but again prefers to live with his wife and gave no further details of himself. Ama is in the rather unusual position of having acquired a farm and house from her father. The father's heir, his brother, is still alive and resides at Akokoaso. He reports that his father came from Ashanti, where he had cocoa farms, to sell rubber, and married a woman from Akokoaso. She only planted food crops at Akokoaso during her lifetime and since she had no daughters, the son claims that he acquired these lands on which the food crops were grown. He himself planted cocoa and also became a timber contractor. When his brother died he acquired his farms which he divided between Ama, because she had looked after her father well, and the other children. Ama herself has seven children, four of whom live with her at Akokoaso, while the other three are married and have migrated. No other persons are living in the house.

The second case also involved a situation where the land being worked came from the wife.

> Akosua Opong lives with her husband in a house which she says belongs to both her and her spouse. Akosua is 45 and has one cocoa farm planted on her land but worked jointly by herself and her husband who has given his own farms to a caretaker. Again there are no further details about the husband. Akosua claims that she acquired her farm from a younger brother of her mother but was reluctant to give any further information. She has four daughters and one son all of whom are working except one who is still at school and lives with her sister in another town. The son is the eldest child and farms on land which he acquired from Akosua's brother. Akosua's 22-year-old daughter is also living in this compound. Before marriage she was growing food crops but now she claims that she is working with her husband on her land.

In both cases, neither spouse appeared to be talking of the establishment of a joint enterprise, nor did they say directly that they were assisting one another. The farms were apparently being developed for the wife; none said they were for the children, and in fact both women had grown children who were working. The comment of one elderly woman who was living with her own and her deceased sister's children is relevant to the position of the men planting on their wives' land. She noted that on the death of her own mother, her sister inherited and, later, she herself inherited. Part of this land was being farmed by her mother's sister's son who lived in the same compound, and the woman commented: 'Can a man take from a woman? If I had asked what would people say?'

Overall production units at Akokoaso were small and hence 60 per cent of all cocoa farm owners reported that they worked independently. Assistance given among married persons was restricted almost entirely to spouses. Male strangers appeared to be in a slightly more enviable position than their local counterparts in this respect, although, as observed already, only one reported that he was assisted by his citizen wife. Unmarried persons, who were mainly women, generally worked on their own; assistance was restricted to their offspring or grandchildren. Thus they relied heavily on hired workers for completing farm work. Offspring who did assist were mostly daughters, but they themselves start producing food crops early in life, particularly once they are married or have children of their own. It must again be remembered therefore that the position of women and relatives as a whole in the labour force may change throughout their life-cycles. Among unmarried women owning cocoa farms, many had been previously married. These women, both local and strangers, were asked about help that they had received in the past, and six out of twenty reported that their husbands had helped them to acquire their own properties. One had been assisted by a son and one had received a farm from a mother's brother. All of the others claimed that they had received no assistance.

RESIDENCE PATTERNS AND ECONOMIC RELATIONSHIPS

Since most male citizens appear to be able to rise to farm ownership over time, it is the varied position of women as assistants, food and cocoa farm owners, that is of particular interest. Women who were assisting their mothers or fathers invariably lived with them even if they were married, whereas the position of assistant to spouse was not necessarily associated with co-residence (Table 3.21). While working for their husbands, wives were just as likely to be living with matrikin or their own parents as to be co-resident with their spouses. It was the young women specialising in food production who were most likely to be residing with their husbands, whereas cocoa farm ownership among women was linked more with separate residence, particularly when the husband was also a citizen. As demonstrated, marital alliances with strangers often resulted in joint conjugal residence. At the same time these women married to strangers were likely to be operating their own cocoa farms, and indeed in some instances to be receiving assistance from their spouses or, as they describe it, to be planting side by side on her land. Finally, consistent with the finding that separate conjugal residence is linked with the greater involvement of women in cocoa

TABLE 3.21 Female Akokoaso citizens among the agricultural labour force by residence and marital alliance

Compound members	Citizen spouse						Stranger spouse				
	Farm owners		Assistants				Farm owners		Assistants		
	Food and cocoa %	Food only %	Assists Spouse %	Mother %	Father %	Hired worker %	Food and cocoa %	Food only %	Assists Spouse %	Mother %	Mother's brother %
Spouse ± offspring	18.2	53.8	45.4	-	-	-	23.5	45.4	-	-	-
Spouse + other	4.5	-	-	-	-	-	17.7	-	-	-	-
Offspring ± grandchildren	22.8	7.7	-	-	-	-	29.4	9.1	-	-	-
Parents/father + siblings	4.5	-	18.2	25.0	100.0	-	-	9.1	-	-	-
Mother + matrikin	50.0	38.5	36.4	75.0	-	100.0	29.4	36.4	100.0	100.0	100.0
Total	100.0	100.0	100.0	100.0	100.0	100.0	100.0	100.0	100.0	100.0	100.0
Number of married female citizens	22	13	11	4	1	1	17	11	1	3	1

production as independent producers, is the finding that it is the unmarried women who are heads of dwelling units who are most likely to own farms.

Almost the whole population of Dominase was working within the agricultural sector but only one-third of the agricultural labour force owned farms. The distribution of farm ownership at Dominase reflected the difficulty of acquiring cultivation rights as strangers which has already been pinpointed at Akokoaso. Again, therefore, the incidence of cocoa farm ownership was greater among citizens than strangers (Table 3.22). In addition farm ownership was almost entirely restricted to men, the majority of women working as assistants although even men were more likely to work as assistants on farms owned by relatives than their Akokoaso counterparts. An important aspect of the role that women appear to be playing in the Dominase area is the almost complete absence of separate food farms. Although at Akokoaso almost two in every three women working within agriculture claimed ownership of a farm, 38 per cent of these specialised in food production.

Again, the changing agricultural roles throughout life are significant. Farm owners were on average older than their assistants and, among the men, were more likely to be married, whereas men assisting relatives, as distinct from hired workers, were more likely to be unmarried (Tables 3.23 and 3.24). Absent from Dominase were the male strangers working on their wives' farms since the migration itself has been largely a male phenomenon. Women came in a supporting capacity as wives rather than to acquire cultivation rights directly themselves. Among women, therefore, cocoa farm ownership was, as at Akokoaso, associated with not being married. Only one of the five female citizens was married and she did not follow her husband. He was a timber worker and did not have any cocoa farms at the site. She says that she arrived at Dominase at the age of thirty-four to 'farm my own land'; previously she had been selling tomatoes at Mim. Another woman did come with her former husband, but again claimed that she was farming her own land. The oldest of the Mim women was sixty and had arrived much later than the others, at the age of fifty-seven. She was related to the chief and was the only one of all the six female owners whose children were all grown and living away. Apart from a tenant labourer in the compound she was living with her seven-year-old grandson. The one stranger among the female owners was also married and came from Berekum town. She first arrived at Dominase with her mother's brother and, when interviewed, was living in a compound built for her by her husband, a citizen. He had a number of wives, all of whom lived in separate compounds. The husband was both a farmer and timber contractor but since all his cocoa farms were mature they were in the hands of caretakers. His wife did little work for him over a twelve-month period and was therefore able to devote all her farming time to the development of her own farms which she had also acquired from her husband.

Male assistants were most likely to be working for their parents and secondly, in the case of Akan men, siblings (Table 3.25). Although there were no Akan males working on a permanent basis for their brothers, brothers did assist one another with labour on a temporary basis and in other ways, as can be seen from the cases

TABLE 3.22 The agricultural labour force at Dominase

	Males				Females			
	Citizens	Strangers			Citizens	Strangers		
		Akan	Non-Akan	Total		Akan	Non-Akan	Total
	%	%	%	%	%	%	%	%
Cocoa farm owners	83.3	55.8	15.0	45.0	35.7	4.2	-	12.8
Assistants								
Assists relative	16.7	32.3	25.0	28.3	64.3	95.8	100.0	87.2
Hired worker	-	11.9	60.0	26.7	-	-	-	-
Total	100.0	100.0	100.0	100.0	100.0	100.0	100.0	100.0
Number of persons	6	34	20	60	14	24	9	47

TABLE 3.23 Farm ownership through life at Dominase

	Males						Females					
	15-24 %	25-44 %	45-64 %	65+ %	NI %	Total %	15-24 %	25-44 %	45-64 %	65+ %	NI %	Total %
Cocoa farm owner[a]	14.3	35.1	84.6	66.7	-	48.3	-	13.0	66.7	-	-	12.8
Assists relative	71.4	29.8	-	33.3	-	25.0	100.0	87.0	33.3	-	100.0	87.2
Hired worker	14.3	35.1	15.4	-	-	26.7	-	-	-	-	-	-
Total	100.0	100.0	100.0	100.0	100.0	100.0	100.0	100.0	100.0	-	100.0	-
Number of persons	7	37	13	3	-	60	17	23	3	-	4	47

NI: No information.

[a] Two also work as caretakers.

TABLE 3.24 Farm ownership at Dominase by citizenship and marital status

	Citizens				Strangers			
	Married		Not married		Married		Not married	
	Males	Females	Males	Females	Males	Females	Males	Females
	%	%	%	%	%	%	%	%
Cocoa farm owners	100.0	10.0	50.0	100.0	44.7	3.1	18.7	-
Assistants								
Assists relative	-	90.0	50.0	-	23.7	96.9	62.6	100.0
Hired worker	-	-	-	-	31.6	-	18.7	-
Total	100.0	100.0	100.0	100.0	100.0	100.0	100.0	100.0
Number of persons	4	10	2	4	38	32	16	1

TABLE 3.25 Relationship of farm owners to assistants at Dominase

Relationship	Citizens		Strangers			
	Married	Not married	Married		Not married	
	Female	Male	Male	Female	Male	Female
	%	%	%	%	%	%
Spouse	88.9			96.8		
Parent	11.1	100.0	66.6	3.2	62.5	100.0
Sibling	-	-	16.7	-	37.5	-
Mother's brother	-	-	16.7	-	-	-
Total	100.0	100.0	100.0	100.0	100.0	100.0
Number of assistants	9	1	6	31	8	1

presented in Chapter 4. Nevertheless brothers were unlikely to continue to assist one another for a long period of time. Among a group of four Ewe brothers, the younger ones had first acquainted themselves with cocoa growing before working as caretakers, receiving a definite share of the crop from their two senior brothers' farms. One had already started to work for himself before the survey ended while the second was about to look for his own piece of land.

Almost all the female assistants were married, and married women were, with one exception, assisting their husbands, even when the husbands were not farm owners. The exception was a young woman recently married whose husband joined her in residence with her mother and stepfather. Although her husband had his own farms, he was also a caretaker and the wife had continued to work for her parents since marriage. In contrast to this situation, one Ewe woman was entirely responsible for her husband's farm while he was away working for a timber company. She was assisted in this work by her husband's brother's son who was twenty-five years old and had come to Dominase less than a year previously. The only other female farm assistant was working for her father.

The distinction in residential arrangements between women as farm owners and women as assistants was even more pronounced at Dominase than at Akokoaso. Thus, all but one of the female heads of residence units were cocoa farm owners. Although two were married, both of the husbands were absent for long periods of time. Generally, women who were co-residing with their spouses were working for them, and thus the position of women at Dominase reflected that of their stranger counterparts at Akokoaso among whom farm ownership was most restricted, and who were also the most likely to be living with their husbands.

MIGRATION AND CHANGE

Although cash cropping, in this instance cocoa farming, has frequently been identified as the main change-inducing feature of the agricultural sector, in fact it would seem that customary economic behaviour persists even in the presence of cash cropping in home territory. The customary pattern of separate residence and production arrangements of spouses continues when both are citizens and have customary access to land. However, when one or both spouses are strangers behaviour patterns show change with co-residence and dependence in economic activities increasing in frequency. Geographical migration is therefore an important constraint on the continuation of customary patterns through space.

Nevertheless, when referring to change, it is necessary to define clearly its nature. At both Akokoaso and Dominase, there was a distinct difference between citizens and strangers in their residential arrangements, the principal feature being the significance of marital ties for determining the residence patterns of strangers. These findings correspond with those of Field (1960) and Fortes (1970) who also observe that in 'new villages', or among 'migrants', the patrilocal residential unit is the more common. This is not, however, a new form of residence and therefore it is the changing distribution of certain residential forms that provides one of the main contrasts between citizens and strangers at Akokoaso and Dominase. Also, fewer persons live under the domestic jurisdiction of female heads at Dominase than at Akokoaso, but women as heads of residence units are still characterised by their unmarried status.

Once the choice of possible residence is restricted, non-customary residential arrangements may however appear. Thus both male and female Akan strangers at Dominase and Akokoaso did co-reside with their spouses and affines. Although migration is a major determinant of residential forms, it does not preclude the influence of other factors, since among Akokoaso citizens there were instances of men living under the domestic jurisdiction of their wives.

The distribution of the agricultural labour force between farm owners and assistants also changes in mobile settings. Thus farm ownership is less widespread among strangers than among citizens. Although both male and female citizens have cultivation rights, wives work on their husbands' farms for at least some time, during which period they may not be in a position to develop their own cocoa farms. Among strangers, wives are particularly isolated in terms of customary relationships since they are more likely to migrate with their husbands than with their own kin or on their own behalf. In addition separate food farming, one of their main concerns at Akokoaso, is not common where cultivation rights have to be purchased. In these situations, therefore, they appear to be at a total disadvantage with respect to farm ownership.

Epstein (1967) and Vercruijsse (1972) each point to the significance of reallocations of the control of resources for changing economic relations and, as demonstrated from the Akokoaso material, particular economic relations do appear to change in these circumstances. Thus as female citizens were placed at an economic advantage relative to their stranger spouses, husbands were working as their assistants. Significant for the interpretation of the position of male strangers working on land belonging to their citizen spouses is the point made by Woodman (1966): that if a male stranger to an area is married to a local woman, it is presumed that he cultivates for the benefit of his children.

Both residence and production patterns vary over a lifetime and this is particularly significant for women. Thus daughters assist and live with their parents when young. At marriage they are likely to work for their husbands although they may also be working on their own food farms. At this time they may, but not necessarily, co-reside with their husbands. Only later do they themselves move into cocoa farm ownership and, associated with this independence, separate residence from their spouse and possibly unmarried status. At this point their offspring are grown and may be relied upon for labour.

At both Akokoaso and Dominase, joint conjugal residence appears to be linked with economic dependence of spouses. This is particularly evident from the Dominase material and among immigrants. Nevertheless, both farms and population at Dominase are comparatively young, and bearing in mind the fact that the position which individuals occupy in the labour force may vary throughout their lives, the development of farms over time needs to be considered. It is obviously important therefore to know more about the content of economic relationships, particularly in mobile settings. The following chapter is concerned with detailing these and total farm investments, since production units alone do not give a comprehensive picture of total farm inputs.

Chapter 4

Investment in cocoa farms

Cocoa farm investments include three main items, land, cash and labour, and it is the sources and allocations of these that are used to begin the investigation of the structural features of cocoa farming already identified at Akokoaso and Dominase.

Information from Akokoaso is presented in the form of a selection of individual reports by farmers on how they acquired their lands and farms, while investment information from Dominase relates to a select group of fifteen Akan farmers and is based on their own reports and on farm management data collected over a twelve-month period for farms located on Dominase land. A number also had farms elsewhere and these are covered in less detail.

ACQUISITION OF COCOA LANDS

Since the Akan make a clear distinction between the soil and its use, when they acquire land, the rights of usufruct are involved. Four main avenues exist by which persons may acquire land as distinct from farms for cocoa farming: by right as citizens of the community in which they are resident, by payment of fees, through gift, and via inheritance.

One of the main advantages of acquiring land in home areas is the fact that no cash payments have to be made. However, family rights in land do exist, at least at Akokoaso, and Beckett (1947) describes how in the 1930s, when the industry was still young, there was a tendency for lineages of the same clan to become neighbouring farmers so that indirect clan rights were assumed. By 1972 few people starting to farm at Akokoaso were able to say, as some older persons did, that the land was there and so they farmed it, and most farmers had acquired their land through inheritance or gift. As noted already, strangers, as is customary, were denied automatic cultivation rights whereas most citizens had land. Citizens acquired cultivation rights by virtue of their membership of a descent group while at the same time parents and spouses each were a further source of farms - as the following report from a female citizen demonstrates.

> At 50 years old, Yaa, the eldest daughter of her mother, has three cocoa farms, one mature and two young ones. She acquired her land from her father who is still alive and living in the same compound. He also has three farms, one planted with cocoa, one with citrus and the third with food crops, on land he says was acquired through his mother's younger brother. Also co-resident is Yaa's brother who works on his father's land, and maintains that in fact his father acquired both his land and farms from a senior brother rather than a mother's brother. Yaa's brother's wife lives in another compound and works separately on land acquired through her mother. Yaa's husband, a citizen, lives in yet another compound and acquired his land through his mother.

Attempts to clarify such issues as through whom people actually acquired their land frequently aroused suspicion, and contradictory statements such as in the case above were therefore left. The story of another woman suggests that it was only sons who were given land by their fathers.

> Ama is 37 years old and says that she planted cocoa and food crops before marrying. She acquired the land through her mother's elder brother and she and her sisters are using this land while her brothers are working on land acquired from their father.

Nevertheless, a number of persons reported that they acquired land from their fathers, although few actually acquired cocoa farms in this way, which corresponds with information given by a number of women who acquired land but not farms from their deceased husbands. A woman of forty, for instance, reported that she worked with her husband when he was alive and was given undeveloped land in return, whereas the cocoa went to his matrikin. Nevertheless she was not planting cocoa on this land 'because I am a woman'. Thus the picture gained was one of endless possibilities and the following case demonstrates that women did acquire developed farms from spouses.

> At 50 years old Efa has three farms all planted with cocoa on land acquired from and planted jointly with her husband. Efa explains that she married young and followed her husband all along. She also has land from her mother's younger brother. Two of her daughters living in the same compound claim to have received farms from their father.

Most frequently people reported that they had acquired farming rights through lineage ties rather than from other sources.

> Kweku is 48 and one of the largest cocoa producers in the village, working on a farm started by his mother. His two citizen spouses have no land of their own and work for him growing food crops while living in a separate compound. When asked about his father's farms, Kweku explains that they were given to his children of whom there are six, who want a surveyor to split the farms before working there. As for his father's sisters sons, he says he knows nothing about them.

Both men and women referred to their mothers when talking of acquiring rights to farm through matrikin. Thus a sixty-four-year-old woman explained that her cocoa farm was acquired from her grandmother who first acquired the land, and a forty-year-old man reported that he had grown food and cocoa on land acquired through his mother. He was formerly a clerk like his father, who migrated from Ashanti and never farmed. His wife was working on the same land as himself, having joined him when her mother's farm had been passed to a caretaker.

At Dominase, all the stranger farmers had acquired cultivation rights by making payments. One citizen farmer, Mr Ahinkurah, was among the fifteen chosen for the in-depth survey (Table 4.1). His case demonstrates clearly the difficulty of farming outside one's usual residence and in frontier areas, even if one is a citizen.

> Mr Ahinkurah came to Dominase at the age of 55 and although he has been trying to establish his 6 acres since 1961 he has not had much success. When he first came, accompanied by his wife, there were many elephants and since there were still few farmers working near his own farm they left for home and returned only four years prior to the survey. Meanwhile his farm was neglected and most of the cocoa had to be replanted when he returned. Even though he is a local man he had to build a compound for himself and the four of his children living with him. In addition he maintains his three older children at Goaso, his home town, with his wife's sister. He uses the proceeds of a self-planted cocoa farm at Goaso and earnings from working as a bricklayer to meet all his expenses since as yet his farms at Dominase are not mature.

Like other citizen farmers at Dominase, Mr Ahinkurah did not talk of acquiring land through successive inheritance nor did he mention particular individuals as being sources of his farms and, overall, it was the farmer as an individual operator that featured strongly in his case.

Although citizens did not make payments for cultivation rights, they, like everyone else, needed to provide shelter for themselves and persons accompanying them, and this part of the settlement cost was high. Estimates made of the cost of establishing 1 acre of cocoa at Dominase indicated that buildings for accommodation alone might comprise one-third of the total cost (Table 4.2). The importance of housing to settlers in pioneer areas is highlighted by the following description by a stranger wife of her arrival at the camp.

> Akosua Addae arrived at the camp in the early 1960s at the age of 29. Her husband and his brothers were the first to leave for Dominase and built part of the house which they are still living in today. Part was given to contract labourers to complete, which they failed to do. Following the husband's return to his home town to harvest the cocoa on a farm he was still caretaking, both she and some annual labourers set off for Dominase and, as Akosua says, they were many at the house. Both she and her husband therefore left the half constructed compound to the annual labourers, and begged a room to sleep in from a neighbour. Akosua

TABLE 4.1 Cash and land resources of fifteen cocoa farmers at Dominase

Age of farm owner on arrival[a]	Settlement assistance received other than contacts	Other current income	Size of farms at Dominase in 1972
Male strangers			Acres
Fifty-three	None	Bearing farm	65.3
Thirty-six	None	Bearing farm	25.1
Forty-three[b]	None	Kente weaver/ bearing farm	39.0
Forty-eight	Inherited farm	Bearing farm	21.4
NA[c]	Inherited farm	Bearing farm	26.2
Twenty-six	Father's farm	Caretaker	15.2
Thirty-three	Land from mother's brother	Store/bearing farm	41.5
Thirty-two	Land from mother's brother	Bearing farm	23.7
Thirty-three	Cheap land	Cocoa buyer	4.8
Twenty-six	Cheap land	Caretaker	6.9
Forty-two	None	Carpenter	6.8
Female strangers			
Thirty[b]	Land from spouse	Trading	4.0
Fifty-four	Land from son	Bearing farm	4.2
Thirty-two	None	Profession	11.4
Male citizen			
Fifty-five	None	Bricklayer/ bearing farm	6.0

NA: Not available.

[a]All ages are approximate.

[b]Refers to age when farms at Dominase acquired.

[c]First owner died just after survey started.

says that she remembers it well because it rained that day but the house was not complete. At that time there were only three buildings at Dominase and the timber contractor who built the road would not allow cars to pass; hence they would walk about 6 miles to find transport to their home town.

TABLE 4.2 Costs of establishing 1 acre of cocoa intercropped at Dominase in 1972

	Cedis
Purchase of cultivation rights[a]	4.00
Buildings to be replaced every ten years[b]	80.00
Tools (axe and cutlass used during establishment years)	9.50
Planting materials:	
300 cocoa pods per acre @ ¢1.50 per 100	4.50
200 plantain suckers per acre @ ¢1.00 per 100	2.00
100 cocoyam corms per acre @ ¢1.00 per 100	1.00
Man-days felling during year 1:	
8.3 man-days @ ¢1.20 per man-day[c]	9.96
Man-days @ ¢0.60 during year 1 (95.4 man-days)	57.24
Man-days @ ¢0.60 during years 2 to 4 (84.0 man-days)	50.40
	¢218.60

[a]Lowest cost per acre recorded in the survey.

[b]These costs should be allocated to whole farms. Since farm size will vary considerably, and some accommodation will be needed regardless of farm size, the total cash cost reported is here allocated to a single acre. Similarly, the total initial investment in land, regardless of when it is planted, should be included in these calculations.

[c]Man-days calculated from published data (Okali, 1975).

Source: Okali (1975), p. 77.

The establishment of farms away from home areas involves therefore a need for cash to settle and, where it involves a stranger, cash to acquire cultivation rights and contacts to introduce the newcomer to the chief. Thus although in theory individuals can operate independently in mobile situations where all inputs including land can be purchased, in practice they need to rely on others. The first stranger farmers who settled at Dominase were invited by the present headman. They included his wife's kinsmen from Berekum town and he himself acted as their intermediary before the Mim chief. It is this need for introductory contacts that in part explains the fact that in 1972 just over half the population of fifteen and over who were not at school had relatives other than spouses living at or near Dominase. The following reports by farmers who provided details of the organisation of their holdings illustrate the importance of ties with relatives, making farm establishment in these pioneer areas possible.

Kwadwo Kusi, Alex Mensah and Kwame Asante were among the few who appeared to have arrived at Dominase relatively independently, the first two relying on bearing farms in their home towns for cash but on relatives for contacts, while Kwame Asante started his first farm elsewhere with the help of his mother's brother. Each had made it possible for other people to settle as cocoa farmers in various places, although Kwadwo Kusi stood out as having assisted many.

> Kwadwo Kusi was among the first group of farmers called by the present headman to settle and arrived at the age of 53 accompanied by his grandson and his sister's daughter's son. The latter had attended school for six years at Berekum, his home town, where he worked as a mason's labourer before joining his grandfather at the age of 18. Kwadwo was able to buy about 70 acres of land with money saved from the produce of his self-acquired bearing farm in his home town, Berekum. He claims that he was receiving up to 400 loads (1) of cocoa from this farm around the time he left, and emphasises that he did not rely on anyone to help him with money since by the time he was ready to ask his uncles for help they had already died. Referring to his farms in his home town he says that since people did not make big farms in any one year, no money was needed to hire labour. Kwadwo's father died when Kwadwo was about 30 years old and his farms went to an elder brother and later on a sister's son, although Kwadwo says that by 1972 the farms were all dead. After they had worked together at Dominase for four years Kwadwo quarrelled with his grandson and purchased a piece of land at Dominase for him to settle on his own. The grandson is still farming on this land and has been joined by a wife from the Central Region who settled at Mim with her mother when she was very young. Kwadwo has since purchased land in the same area for three sisters on behalf of their sons, and two others have been given part of the farm which he himself is developing. In addition he has purchased a separate plot of land at a nearby site for one of his own sons and has given his other offspring part of the 70 acres which he is developing since, as he himself remarks, one brother will not care for it and then share it out.

Also among the first to be called from Berekum to settle was Alex Mensah.

> Alex Mensah, the eldest son of his mother, was only 36 when he left home to work on Dominase land, using the proceeds of a

---

1 A load of cocoa is 60 lb.

bearing farm in his home town. In his case, however, production was about 50 loads at the time and he only purchased about 30 acres of land. He has given part of this to his sister's son who works with him at Dominase and gave another piece of land to a younger brother who joined him later. Mr Mensah is preparing to return to his home town to plant cocoa on land provided by his mother's brother, having planted all his land at Dominase.

Kwame Asante, a farmer and Kente weaver, lives in Kumasi while two of his sons have been responsible for developing his farms at Dominase. One of these, Kwabena, has spent the last six years working for his father and reported on his father's farming activities. Kwame has four farms each in a different locality and all outside his home town. The first of these was established on land provided by his mother's brother in return for help which he had given him. As Kwabena remarks, those who helped him he helped in return. Kwame arrived at Dominase at the age of 43 and purchased about 39 acres. The farm was first started by Kwabena's younger brother who has since been settled independently elsewhere in the district by his father. Just before the survey ended, Mr Asante also purchased a separate piece of land at Dominase for Kwabena which he plans to plant while at the same time continuing with the work he is doing now.

Kwesi Poku is the last example of those who had both established themselves and provided land for other people during their lifetimes, but he had to seek financial assistance from matrikin before settling. Kwesi arrived at Dominase at the same time as Kwadwo Kusi and Alex Mensah, at the age of forty-eight.

Kwesi has two farms in his home town, one established by himself which was producing 200 loads when he came to farm on Dominase land, and a farm he inherited from his only uterine brother. He has no uterine sisters but has given land to three of his mother's sister's children and claims that he has asked others to join him at New Berekum but they have refused. For himself he purchased about 21 acres. Kwesi says that he also had to borrow money to meet his costs when he came and this he did from his mother's sister who had cared for him when his own mother died.

The position of nephews who have received undeveloped land from their uncles is demonstrated by Kwame Ayim and Kwabena Danso, although both had bearing farms of their own in their home towns before moving to work at Dominase.

Mr Ayim arrived at Dominase in 1959 at 32 years of age with three of his brothers, and his mother's brother's son, all of whom were being provided with land by the latter's father. Two of the brothers later returned home to care for the same uncle's farm, while Mr Ayim and one other brother remained at Dominase. The two brothers live in the same compound but do not share any business interests or assist one another on their farms in any way. Mr Ayim has been able to plant 42 acres of cocoa on this land over eleven years and has in addition a number of other cocoa farms. The first was established by himself in his home town where he also acquired another from his father's sister's son as pledge for a loan not repaid. He also purchased just over 4 acres of land at Dominase but by this time the land in the immediate vicinity was finishing. In 1972 therefore when his mother's brother came again to purchase land for him, it was land lying a few miles away which was finally acquired. This time however Mr Ayim was not prepared to accept the offer, preferring to pay for his own piece himself. In doing so he remarked that if he did not he might soon find himself establishing cocoa for the whole family alone. Mr Ayim has reached a position where he can in fact operate independently with respect to further investment in land. In addition to his farms he also owns a store and drinking bar and in 1972 when his mother's brother had a car accident following a visit to Dominase he gave him a substantial amount for repairs.

The behaviour of Mr Ayim following his own successful farm establishment will be discussed in detail later. Mr Danso was a younger man who had also established cocoa on land purchased by his mother's brother and some which he purchased himself, a total of 24 acres. Although he also had a bearing farm in his home town, another piece of land was purchased on his behalf by the same uncle in 1971, which he did not refuse.

The remaining farmers had received less substantial and frequently more indirect help than Kwame Ayim or Kwabena Danso. None had reached the stage of actually settling others independently. The first, Kofi Owusu, died two months after the survey started and at a time when he had just reached the stage of being able to help others. Like Kwesi Poku, Mr Owusu used the proceeds of two bearing farms in his home town, one planted himself, the other inherited, to start his first farm on Dominase land with a brother. Kofi was in his early fifties at the time and his heir, a sister's son, had earlier suggested that he follow him to the Trans Bia area but Kofi did not have enough money at the time. In total, he and his brother established almost 11 acres on Dominase land, all of which Kofi inherited at his brother's death. He purchased a further 16 acres of land eight years after he had first arrived but unfortunately died before this area was firmly established.

In the remaining cases of the male strangers, all, like Mr Akinkurah, the citizen, were continuing with work that they were doing before arriving at Dominase or had another source of income that they were using for farm establishment.

Kweku Amoa was first brought to Dominase by his mother's brother, Kwame Asante, although he paid for the land himself. Kweku was only in his mid-twenties when he arrived and purchased about 15 acres of land using proceeds from a farm which he was caretaking along with his brothers, and which still occupies his time for a large part of the year. His farm at Dominase has not been very successful and since only about half of it is mature, the rest still being young cocoa among food crops, his main interest continues to lie with the other farm, from which he gains his most substantial income.

The remaining farmers had purchased smaller acreages of land and in each case they were just starting their cocoa holdings.

> Mr Obese has almost 7 acres of land which he is in the process of establishing. His is the most distant farm from the camp site and he is one of the few farmers who appears to be gaining little from the food crops planted on the young cocoa farms. In addition to his farming Mr Obese also works as a carpenter for whose services there is a fairly heavy demand, while his wife works as a farm labourer at various times throughout the year to earn additional income.

Mr Okai and Mr Ayesi were more recent arrivals at Dominase and were therefore facing land shortages and, as a result, increased land prices. Mr Okai had previously worked as a clerk and store-keeper and was earning an income as a cocoa buyer during the cocoa season while establishing his farms at Dominase. Mr Ayesi had spent most of his time farming and used the proceeds from his work as a caretaker of a bearing farm for making his land purchase. Since he was continuing this work he travelled from Dominase during the cocoa season. Although 4 acres of Mr Ayesi's cocoa had started to bear by the time the survey ended, this was not sufficient for his needs and he hired a caretaker to complete the harvest while he travelled to caretake elsewhere. In doing this, Mr Ayesi was not following the usual pattern of farm establishment where, at least at this site, the farmers themselves, or at least a relative, looked after the farms until they were mature. Both Mr Okai and Mr Ayesi had received assistance from matrikin who had sold land to them at a price far lower than it would have been had they bought from the chief. Mr Okai also received additional help from his mother's brother who permitted him to pledge a farm to furnish the cash that enabled him to register as a cocoa buyer. Towards the end of the survey Mr Okai purchased a second plot of land for which his sister provided half the money from her trading activities. Mr Okai was also the only farmer among the fifteen who received some assistance, albeit indirect, from his wife's kin, who were citizens. He engaged in timber work, which is reserved for Mim people, to earn some extra money, but in order to do this he worked jointly with his wife's sister. Like Mr Ayesi, Mr Okai relied heavily on his income from cocoa buying, plus the food crops taken from his young farms, to live. In total he had managed to acquire almost 5 acres of land with his first purchase and Mr Ayesi, 7 acres.

Mr Obese, also from Berekum town, had experienced the most difficulties, arriving comparatively late in life at the age of forty-two to start his first cocoa farm.

The previous analysis of Dominase residents suggested that women were less likely to acquire lands in the pioneer areas than men. Only six women were found to be farming independently and five of these were from Mim. Four were unmarried, three of whom had travelled to the site independently, while the fourth had arrived at Dominase with her husband who had since died.

Three of the fifteen farmers working on Dominase land were women who did little or no work for other people. None were citizens, only one was resident at Dominase itself and each had acquired her farms in a different way.

Adjoa Owusuwa's story provides an example of one of the most frequently cited methods of a woman acquiring farms: from her husband.

> Adjoa was 26 when she first arrived to farm with her mother's brother after living with her mother's sister following the death of her parents. A year later Adjoa married a man who already had a number of wives, only one of whom was also living at Dominase. Both wives shared the same compound for one year after which a second was built. Adjoa's husband, a citizen, is over 60 and has a number of mature cocoa farms which he has given to caretakers, while at the same time he works as a timber contractor and spends little time at Dominase itself. Adjoa worked only six days on her husband's farm over the twelve-month survey period, and was able to devote most of her working time to the development of her own separate business activities. These include a 4-acre cocoa farm, which she is developing on land provided by her husband, and trading, which again was started with money from her husband. During her six years of marriage Adjoa has had three children and is expecting another. Although she has a number of matrikin living close by, few visit her and on the birth of her children, her only sister who still lives in their home town comes to help. Adjoa's closest relative, the person on whom she says she would rely most, is a brother now living overseas.

The customary practice of husbands giving wives land or farms involves the consent of the donor's matrikin and confirmation of the gift by an aseda payment from the beneficiaries to them. Adjoa had not yet completed any of these formal arrangements. In addition, Adjoa was in a different position from most women in that she had received farms without having actually developed those of her husband. As we shall see later, most women acquiring farms from their spouses receive these at least partly in return for labour given on his farms.

Yaa Asabea, the second woman, was much older and in a completely different position from Adjoa.

> Yaa is 60 years old and lives in her compound with her granddaughter; a farm labourer is a tenant in the compound. All Yaa's children are grown. One, a daughter, lives in an adjacent compound with her husband, Mr Mensah, and his two other wives; one son works for a timber company while also farming at Dominase. A second son lives in her home town. Yaa has been trying somewhat unsuccessfully to establish a 4-acre cocoa farm on Dominase land for five years. The land was purchased for her by one of her two sons. Yaa has a farm in her home town which she says she started with her grandmother following the death of Yaa's husband. According to Yaa, the husband refused to transfer anything to her before he died and so she got nothing. Yaa appeared to rely heavily on her children for her income. Among all the farmers she was the most reluctant to provide regular information about her farming activities and did not wish to discuss her relatives, her main fear being that she might lose the farm which she had worked so hard to acquire.

The last woman, Akosua Koarantema, lived at Mim town with her children while her husband resided in Kumasi. Akosua did not actively farm herself but is probably one of the few professional women who has actually invested in cocoa farming. Her farm was already planted, although neglected, when she purchased it. Most of her money had been spent replanting sections and maintaining the rest.

Four other women, although not working independently on a full-time basis, had also started farms with the help of their husbands. Alex Mensah's three wives were cultivating approximately 2 acres for themselves which was part of the 25 acres he was developing. They had also been promised part of a young bearing farm on the same land but when pressed about this Mr Mensah asked 'Can a woman own land?' Mr Ahinkurah's wife, a citizen like himself, was just starting her own separate farm and was hiring labour with the proceeds of a bearing farm which she and her siblings were given by their father's heir, while her husband was also assisting.

Problems over conflicting claims to the same piece of land increased the farmers' reliance on others at Dominase. Kwadwo Kusi, for instance, paid £160 for a piece of land for one of his sister's sons, the ownership of which was disputed. The land was finally auctioned by the chief and reclaimed by Kwadwo himself at the auction price.

The information from both Akokoaso and Dominase demonstrates the importance of relatives for both citizen and stranger farmers. Although ties with matrikin were particularly important at Akokoaso, citizens had acquired land and farms from a wide variety of persons including matrikin, parents and spouses and it was the numerous possible sources of both land and farms that was significant. At Dominase, both citizens and strangers were migrants in the sense of living outside their home towns, and strangers could purchase cultivation rights, making individual access to resources possible in theory. In practice, ties with relatives were equally necessary to ensure success in a situation involving considerable risk and uncertainty. Thus although Mr Ahinkurah had arrived to settle with no direct assistance from matrikin, he, like Mr Obese, the stranger, had not had much success. Among the strangers, the majority had received some assistance. For men, it was their mothers' brothers who featured prominently. Among the women, most of whom were not yet working entirely on their own, it was their husbands, although offspring were important for Yaa Asabea. It is the stranger married to a citizen who introduces a new relationship, that of a man with his affines, and thus Mr Okai was able to profit from his local ties. This did not mean, however, that he was working to establish any joint farm with his affines, or, as will be shown later, with his wife.

Mr Poku and Mr Owusu had both used the proceeds from inherited farms to support their settlement at Dominase. As was noted in the discussion of the Akan, writers are not in agreement as to whether the use of such funds results in the formation of a corporate concern, and again therefore these two farmers were not operating in situations that clearly separated them from customary ties.

The ability of individuals to operate without reference to descent groups depends mainly on their ability to operate in the open market and a number of farmers were investing money earned in other occupations in their farms. Nevertheless, this was in addition to, rather than instead of, relying on the assistance of matrikin and others.

LAND DEVELOPMENT

Apart from spraying machines that are needed to combat pests, the most important production factor needed by cocoa farmers for land development is labour. Labour costs at Dominase were estimated to comprise just over half the total costs during the first two years of farm establishment and just less than half in years 5 to 12 (Tables 4.2 and 4.3). (2) In terms of total labour requirements, the first year of farm establishment is the most expensive, while mature farms require the least man-days. Thus it is when a farmer is just starting his farm that his labour demands are heaviest.

TABLE 4.3 Annual costs incurred on 1 acre of bearing cocoa years 5 to 12 at Dominase

Item	Cost cedis
Rent for land use @ 1/10 returns[a]	6.96
Tools (cutlasses only)	2.00
Spraying @ ¢1.80 twice yearly	3.60
Man-days @ ¢0.60 per man-day for 17.7 man days	10.62
Total	23.18

[a] Beginning at year 13, for purposes of calculating the present value of future returns, it was assumed that yield reaches a maximum of ten loads per acre, and harvesting data and rent were adjusted accordingly. If the cost of food and drinks incurred during cocoa-breaking operations is used instead of man-days, the results are similar. The 1972 price of ¢12.00 per 60 lb load of dry cocoa is used.

Source: Okali (1975), p. 78.

Peak work-loads during the first year occur in March and June when fifteen seven-hour man-days per acre are required. An individual can therefore only operate alone if he is starting a small farm. Once account is taken of sickness and other work, even this is difficult to achieve and, on average, only in three individual months of the year did any one male farm owner or on-site manager work fifteen actual days or more on the Dominase farms.

Since farms and holdings are developed gradually over time, it is

2 Information on labour and cash requirements for cocoa farming at Dominase is taken from Okali (1975).

the cumulative work-load that gives a clearer indication of labour requirements. Thus in the first year 101 man-days are required per acre, in the second 31, and 18 on a mature farm. In total, to work on 3 acres of different ages would require 132 man-days with a maximum of 21 during peak working months.

Obviously in a situation where labour can be hired it is possible to conceive of individuals working without relatives, thus avoiding altogether any possible conflicts arising from spouses, offspring and descent group members each having invested in a single farm. As will be seen in the analysis, this rarely occurs, one of the reasons being that finances are not unlimited and relatives are not necessarily compensated with cash and, even if they are, they may not be paid immediately. That this is not the only important factor is suggested by the wealthier farmers, each of whom did not rely solely on hired labour.

Critical for the analysis of the labour data is the difference in types of work required on farms of different ages. Three categories of farms have been distinguished: those planted during the survey period in 1971 and 1972 and referred to as 'new' - data cover the first twelve months of establishment; farms containing trees thirteen months to full bearing age and referred to as 'young' - these actually included trees varying in age from 13 months up to five calendar years; and finally 'bearing' farms that contained trees of five to twelve calendar years at the start of the survey. One of the main differences between these farms is the amount of time spent on food crops interplanted with the cocoa. Within the first year of farm establishment, approximately one-quarter of the total time was used for planting and harvesting the major shade crop plantain and other food items, compared with only 5 per cent on young farms and less than a whole working day on bearing farms. On all farms the most time-consuming activity was weeding, which accounted for 35, 84 and 41 per cent of the time spent on the new, young and bearing farms respectively.

SOURCES OF LABOUR

Farm management data for Akokoaso were collected by Beckett (1947) in the 1930s. They provide only a general description of labour arrangements on farms at the time with distinctions made between the farmer and his family, including wives and children and possibly others, none of whom were specified, and hired workers (Beckett, 1947). Ten Akan male farmers, including one stranger, were selected. All but two of the farms were planted by the owners themselves. Data were collected over a period of three years and covered only two categories of farms, bearing and non-bearing, the latter including those where food crops were still grown and corresponding to the new and young farms referred to in the analysis of the Dominase data. The main finding relevant to the present analysis is that wives and children, possibly with other relatives, were the main source of labour for all the ten farmers.

The fifteen farmers working on Dominase land relied on a wide variety of relatives both on their farms at Dominase and farms located elsewhere (Tables 4.4 and 4.5a and b). In total, they were operating forty-three farms as separate units at Dominase while nine farmers also had mature bearing farms, most of which were in their home towns.

Excluding hired workers, the total permanent labour force working on the farms at Dominase in 1971 was fifteen men and twenty women; and including the permanent hired workers, the labour force was thirty men and twenty women. Permanent workers included caretakers and annual labourers. Caretakers specialised in working on bearing farms although they did assist briefly with work on other farms, whereas annual labourers were employed to work on new farms. Among the fourteen hired labourers employed at the beginning of the survey period three were annual labourers, one assisting on a new farm being started by Kwabena Asante's son and two working for Akosua Korantema, the absent female owner. By 1972, the number of hired labourers had increased to sixteen, among whom were four annual labourers. The labour situation on farms was changing throughout the survey period; once farms reached maturity they were passed to hired caretakers, allowing the farm owners to concentrate on expanding their holdings. Although wives of caretakers did assist briefly during cocoa harvesting, they did not complete any other major tasks on farms and could not therefore be regarded as permanent assistants in any sense. Thus they are not included in the total.

Three farm owners lived far from the site, including Akosua Korantema who came regularly to check on the work done on her farms and in this way tried to manage the farms herself. Kwame Asante's son Kwabena was working as farm manager on his father's behalf and his duties included hiring and supervising the work of hired labourers and providing labour himself. Mr Asante did no work on the farms and rarely visited Dominase. It was his son who regularly travelled to Kumasi to report on what was happening at the farm camp, and who decided, for instance, that the new acreage they had planned to plant in 1971 should be reduced.

Kofi Owusu died at the beginning of the survey, prior to which he was assisted by a number of relatives, including his eldest son who was married. The heir, who had farms elsewhere, retained this son as manager of all his inherited properties at Dominase. These included two bearing farms, and for this work the son was given a caretaker contract for one-third of the proceeds. Mr Owusu's farms were, however, divided among various persons following his death - including his senior son, his two wives, a sister's son and the heir. All but the heir worked on the farms both prior to and after his death but only the son resided near Dominase throughout.

Overall, excluding the hired workers, wives were the main source of permanent labour assisting the male farmers, including owners or their on site managers, at Dominase. However, wives were unlikely to be helping husbands in their capacity as assistants while the owners themselves were present. Thus, although both Mr Kusi's son and Mr Mensah's sister's son were married and worked as permanent assistants for their father and mother's brother respectively, their wives did not work with them. Among the owners with bearing farms at Dominase, four had more than one wife assisting and two others had second wives in their home towns - although one of the latter did work at Dominase prior to the survey but left following a disagreement with her husband. All of the six resident male owners with bearing farms had therefore more than one wife.

TABLE 4.4 Composition and management of farms at Dominase, 1971-2

Age and sex of farmer[c]		Relation to owner	Farms at Dominase Acres			Years planted			Acres	
			Bearing	Young	New	Bearing	Young	New	1971	1972
Sixty-five	M	Owner	37.7	23.5	1.9 2.2	1959-66	1969-70	1971 1972	37.7	37.7
Forty-five	M	Owner	15.7 4.0	2.2 2.2	1.0	1959-64	1968-9	1972	15.7	15.7
Twenty-two	M	Son	30.5		8.5	1963-9		1971	30.5	30.5
Sixty	M	Owner	17.0		3.9 0.5	1959		1971 1972	17.0	17.0
Thirty-six	M	Part owner[b]	10.7	11.0	4.5	1961-8	1969-70	1971		
Thirty-six	M	Owner	7.8	4.5	0.8 2.1	1961	1969	1971 1972	7.8	7.8
Forty-five	M	Owner	37.2		2.7 1.6	1959-70		1971 1972	37.2	37.2
Forty	M	Owner	8.6	10.9	1.8 2.4	1963-6	1969-70	1971 1972		8.6
Thirty-five	M	Owner		1.2	1.7 1.9		1970	1971 1972		
Thirty	M	Owner		4.3	2.6		1967-70	1971		
Forty-five	M	Owner		3.3	1.0 2.5		1968-70	1971 1972		
Sixty-five	M	Owner		5.2	0.8		1961-71	1972		

Thirty-two	F	Owner	1.6	0.4 2.0	1970	1971 1972
Sixty	F	Owner	4.2		1966-71	
NA	M[a]	Hired worker	11.4		1969-71	

NA: Not available.

[a]The female owner lives and works in non-farm occupation in Mim town.

[b]Also manages on behalf of father's heir.

[c]Farmers refer to owners or on-site managers. Farm managers working in the absence of owners hire labour, purchase inputs and frequently also provide labour themselves.

ʌBLE 4.5a Labour force on farms located at Dominase in 1971 and 1972

ɟe and ːx of ɩrmer		Permanent relatives				Temporary relatives						Hired[a] workers	Size of Dominase farms
			Offspring			Offspring							
		Spouse	Male	Female	Sister's son	Male	Female	Nephew	Father's sister's son	Sib-lings	Mother		
.xty-five	M	2	1									2	65.3
ɾorty-five	M	3			1							2	25.1
Twenty-one[b]	M	1	1			1						3	39.0
Sixty	M	1						2[c]				2	21.4
Thirty-six[d]	M	1							1	1	2		26.2
Thirty-six	M	1										1	15.2
Forty-five	M	2						1				2(3)	41.5
Forty	M	2(1)		1(0)	1(0)					1	1	(1)	23.7
Thirty-five	M	1								2			4.8
Thirty	M	1											6.9
Forty-five	M	1					1						6.8
Sixty-five	M	1					1						6.0
Thirty-two[e]	F												4.0
Sixty	F					1	1						4.2
NA[f]	M											2	11.4

NA: Not available.

[a]Permanent labourers only.

[b]The owner did not work on the farms and spouse refers to son's wife.

[c]Nephew in this case includes one brother's son and one mother's sister's son.

[d]This farmer is only part owner of the holding. He acts as manager for his father's heir who has never worked on the farms. Persons assisting are defined by their relationship to this manager.

[e]Spouse also worked one day for wife.

[f]The owner herself did not work on the farms and hired two permanent labourers.

TABLE 4.5b Labour force on farms outside Dominase, 1971-2

Age of farm owner in 1971		Person in charge/ relation to owner	Source of farms
Sixty-five	M	Daughter and son-in-law	Self-planted
Forty-five	M	Hired caretakers	Self-planted
Fifty-one	M	Mother's brother and brother	Self-planted
Sixty	M	Hired caretakers	Self-planted and inherited
NA	M	Mother's brother's son	Inherited
Thirty-six	M	No farm	-
Forty-five	M	Father's sister's son	Self-planted and pledge
Forty	M	Sister's son	Self-planted
Thirty-five	M	No farm	-
Thirty	M	No farm	-
Forty-five	M	No farm	-
Sixty-five	M	Self	Self-planted
Thirty-two	F	No farm	-
Sixty	F	Son	Self and grandmother
NA	F	No farm	-

NA: Not available.

After wives, offspring featured most prominently in the permanent labour force, one daughter and two sons, including Kwame Asante's son. Offspring were significant even in the case of Kwadwo Kusi, who had assisted a large number of matrikin to acquire farms and who was accompanied originally by his sister's daughter's son. Mr Kusi provides an interesting contrast with Mr Mensah. Both had numerous adult offspring, but whereas Mr Kusi relied entirely on them for labour, Mr Mensah's children never worked on his farms either at Dominase or in his home town. Mr Mensah was the only farmer who relied on a sister's son on a permanent basis to act both as farm manager in his absence and provide labour. He was also selling cocoa on Mr Mensah's behalf and preparing to plant his own farm at the end of the survey period.

Only Mr Danso was assisted by both offspring, a daughter and a sister's son, at the same time on the same site, although Mr Owusu also was assisted before he died. Neither assistant was married and in this respect differed from the other assistants. Both left at a later date, the daughter to marry, and the sister's son because Mr Danso was dissatisfied with his work. Although only one sister's son is noted in Table 4.5a as working for Mr Danso on a permanent basis, he was sent others later and had tried a number previously. Mr Danso's senior wife departed with her daughter and although he later married again, at this point he hired a caretaker to work on his bearing farm. Among the eight farmers with bearing farms at Dominase, Mr Danso was one of the two, including Kofi Owusu's son acting as manager on behalf of his father's heir, who was initially not relying on hired permanent assistants.

There was a distinct difference in labour sources between farmers just starting their cocoa and those expanding existing holdings. Wives were the only source of permanent workers for the on-site owners with young holdings. Once bearing farms were included, the permanent labour force was enlarged both by the addition of other relatives and hired workers. Among the nine owners with bearing farms either on Dominase land or elsewhere, only Mr Ahinkurah, Kwesi Poku and Kweku Amoa did not include relatives other than wives, and even then Kwesi's brother's sons and mother's sisters' sons assisted temporarily and Mr Ahinkurah's daughter worked one day. Mr Poku's position differed from that of the other men at Dominase in that he lacked close male matrikin. His parents divorced when he was young and, when his mother died soon after, he was cared for by his mother's sister. Kwesi's only brother also died and since he had no sisters or mother's brothers, the only persons on whom he could rely for labour were nephews who were reluctant to stay permanently with him on his farms at Dominase. Kweku Amoa had the smallest bearing acreage, about 8, and was also the youngest owner among the group with bearing farms. He was still involved in caretaking a farm elsewhere and did not appear to be in a position to request others to help him at Dominase.

Although the data for farms located at other sites, which were in all cases bearing, refer only to the main person in control, and are not based on detailed work records, it is possible to see that relatives still feature significantly in the production unit as a whole. Here, however, they are working mainly as supervisors since all but Mr Ahinkurah's farm had been handed to a caretaker. In the case of Mr Kusi it was his daughter and son-in-law who were working as caretakers.

Almost all the male farmers received some temporary assistance from persons other than their wives on the Dominase farms. Only Kweku Amoa and Yaw Ayesi did not, and both of these men were working as caretakers at another site where they spent a number of months throughout the year. Among these assistants, matrikin were particularly important, including siblings, in two cases sisters, and in one both a brother and sister. It is interesting to note that the one citizen, Mr Ahinkurah, did not appear to have received any more assistance than other persons and his daughter's contribution, as already stated, amounted in total to only three hours over twelve months.

Of the three female owners, only Akosua Korantema, the absentee farmer, relied on permanent assistants; these were hired workers. She had no adult offspring and no one related to her worked permanently on farms. Yaa Asabea, an older woman, received some temporary assistance from two of her three married offspring, one of whom, a daughter, was living in a nearby compound. Adjoa Owusuwa, the younger woman living on the site, had only three small children and could not therefore rely on them for help. Her own husband, who spent little time at Dominase and hired labourers to work on his own farm, went to farm with his wife for one day over the twelve months. The three wives working on land provided by their husbands also received no help from relatives although all had grown children. Mr Ahinkurah's wife started her farm at the end of the survey and it was not possible therefore to know his contribution.

Overall, persons other than matrikin were the most important sources of permanent labour on the farms at Dominase for male owners and managers. However, among the persons who assisted temporarily, matrikin featured more prominently while the more mature farms elsewhere were supervised by a variety of persons, including caretakers and, in Mr Ayim's case, his father's sister's son.

Although it was the men with the younger holdings who relied almost exclusively on wives, no male farmer was unaccompanied by a spouse, and among those with older holdings, a number had more than one wife at the site. As was suggested in Chapter 3, it was the women that were least likely to be receiving assistance from relatives in the form of labour and who therefore relied most on hired labour.

THE USE OF LABOUR

Only when the actual amount and type of work completed by members of the labour force is considered can a full picture of the contributions made be gained. Beckett (1947) recorded at Akokoaso that

> The total work done in the farms by wives and children is greater than that by the farmer himself, and it will be noted that whereas two thirds of the family work is done on the non-bearing farms, the farmer puts in twice as much time in his bearing cocoa as in his young farms. (Beckett, 1947: 87).

The amount of work that different members of the labour force completed on the farms at Dominase varied considerably (Table 4.6). On farms owned by men, wives, like their husbands, completed almost a quarter of the work. The contribution of other persons was on the whole small, even though they were almost equal in number. Female farmers, in contrast, completed half the total farm work themselves while hired labourers completed most of the remainder.

As observed already, where the farm owners were absent, and persons other than hired labourers were in charge, it was the farm manager and his wife who completed most of the work (Table 4.7a and b).

Although wives completed fewer hours on average than their husbands, individually their contributions varied greatly and in three cases exceeded that of their husbands. However, it should be remembered that reference is being made here only to work on farms and only those on Dominase land, and the amount of work that persons can do on farms depends on the other things that they may have or wish to do. Having more than one wife did not necessarily therefore mean that the amount of work done was increased likewise. In only

TABLE 4.6 Contribution of labour to work on farms at Dominase, June 1971-May 1972

	Men's farms[a] %	Women's farms %
Male farmer	23.4	-
Female farmer	-	49.5
Offspring	3.0	6.1
Spouse	23.4	0.1
Female matrikin	1.5	-
Male matrikin	7.6	-
Other farmers	7.5	-
Casual hired labour	13.6	41.7
Permanent hired labour	20.0	2.6
Total	100.0	100.0
Number of hours	31,445	3,734

[a]Excludes one farm where the data for young and new farms were combined.

Note: Includes only the farms where the owner was also the on-site manager. Among the women's farms is that being operated by Mr Mensah's three wives.

two of the four cases where more than one wife helped on the farms at Dominase did this occur. Mr Mensah's wives, for instance, each worked a different number of hours, and on average did less work on their husband's farms than all the wives. Among the remaining male farmers, Kwabena Danso's wives did the most work and Kwesi Poku's among the least. Kwesi Poku's junior wife gave birth to twins just before the survey started and his senior wife had returned home. Other women also had children during the survey, including Kwame Ayim's senior wife - and in her case she did less farm work than any since she spent a number of months in hospital. Her co-wife, however, made up for this loss and together they completed more than double that of Mr Poku's single wife. One of the advantages of having more than one wife would appear to be that of reducing the risk of total loss of assistance when one is sick or unavailable for other reasons, rather than to increase the total work done. Mr Mensah's senior wife, for instance, did only half the farm work of the junior wife at Dominase and spent more time than any of the three in her home town, but at least one wife was always at the Dominase farm site.

Among relatives other than wives, the contributions varied greatly. Mr Mensah's sister's son only worked sixty-eight man-days which was among the lowest recorded for any of the permanent assistants. In contrast, Mr Danso's sister's son completed more hours

TABLE 4.7a Contribution of labour to work on farms at Dominase, June 1971-May 1972

Age and sex of farm owner		Opening acreage			Own labour			Male matrikin			Offspring			Spouse			Female matrikin		
		B	Y	N	B	Y	N	B	Y	N	B	Y	N	B	Y	N	B	Y	N
Sixty-five	M	37.7	23.5	1.9	70	986		-	-	-	8	555		(2) 129	1,744		-	-	-
Forty-five	M	19.7	4.4[a]		566	21	33	359	-	50	-	-	-	(3) 814	750	123	-	-	-
Sixty	M	17.0		3.9	248	29	520	138	308	45	-	-	-	(1) 37	6	257	-	-	-
Thirty-six	M	7.8	4.5	0.8	148		399		-					(1) 76	72	576			
Forty-five	M	37.2		2.7	503	34	267	72[b]	-	131[b]	-	-	-	(2) 200	88	478	14	-	-
Forty	M	8.6	10.9	1.8	222	649	389	240	753	113	101	567	199	(2) 250	1,114	713	27	105	172
Thirty-five	M		1.2	1.7		122	750		43	123				(1)	125	400		27	120
Thirty	M		4.3	2.6		233	320							(1)	119	394			
Forty-five	M		3.3	1.0		682	261					18	56	(1)	251	634			
Sixty-five	M		5.2			552	407						3	(1)	205	346			
Thirty-two	F		1.6	0.4		83	405									4			
Sixty	F		4.2			686						229							

Age and sex of farm owner		Other farmers			Hired casual labour			Hired caretakers			Annual labour			Total hours			Closing acreage		
		B	Y	N	B	Y	N	B	Y	N	B	Y	N	B	Y	N	B	Y	N
Sixty-five	M	540		110	66	3,786		2,096	24		-	-	-	2,916	7,198		37.7	25.4	2.2
Forty-five	M	654	-	-	327	288	126	1,634	-	-	-	-	-	4,354	1,059	332	19.7	4.4	1.0
Sixty	M	425			102	90	450	1,403						2,353	433	1,272	17.0	3.9	0.5
Thirty-six	M	225		2	6	24	150	834						1,289	96	1,361	7.8	5.3	2.1
Forty-five	M	726			240	42	778	1,942	48	12		24	48	3,697	236	1,714	37.2	2.7	1.6
Forty	M	194	50		72	202	168		28	90				1,106	3,468	1,844	8.6	12.7	2.4
Thirty-five	M			101		186	276								503	1,770		2.9	1.9
Thirty	M					234									586	714		6.9	
Forty-five	M					324	162								1,275	1,113		4.3	2.5
Sixty-five	M					156									913	756		5.2	0.8
Thirty-two	F					282	834		96						461	1,243		2.0	2.0
Sixty	F					316									1,231			4.2	

[a] Includes one young farm being worked separately by the three wives.

[b] Labour completed by one boy later described as 'someone from a nearby house' in the home town.

Notes:
1 This table was published in a more simplified form in Okali (1975), pp. 40-1.
2 Includes only farms where the owner was also the on-site manager. The remaining farms are covered in Table 4.7b.
3 B refers to bearing, Y to young and N to new farms.
4 Figures in brackets for wives refers to the number of wives assisting in 1971.

TABLE 4.7b Labour force on farms at Dominase for absentee owners, 1971-2

Relation to manager	Kwame Asante's farms			Kofi Owusu's farms			Akosua Korantema's farm
	B	Y	N	B	Y	N	Y
Opening acreage	30.5		8.5	10.7	11.0	4.5	11.4
Manager[a]	15	336	654	667	505	194	-
Wife	6	235	324	404	454	254	-
Sister	-	-	-	-	7	-	-
Mother/father's wife	-	-	-	22	12	245	-
Father's sister's son	-	-	-	20	-	181	-
Wife of father's sister's son	-	-	-	4	-	142	-
Other farmers	-	-	-	230	-	-	-
Hired casual labour	792	78	1,068	366	834	96	214
Hired caretakers	2,189	-	456	-	-	-	595
Annual labour	5	284	705	-	-	-	1,222
Total hours	3,007	933	3,207	1,713	1,812	1,112	2,031
Closing acreage	30.5	8.5		10.7	15.5		11.4

[a] Kofi Owusu's son was also part owner.

than anyone else, followed by his daughter. Among the temporary assistants it was his own mother who worked most. Although the total number of hours completed on Mr Danso's farms ranked the third largest, he relied on hired workers least of all the farmers. His position changed radically following the departure of his senior wife accompanied by her daughter.

In general temporary assistants contributed little. Adjoa Owusuwa's husband went to her farm one day, as did Mr Ahinkurah's daughter. Yaa Asabea's daughter did five days' work while her son, even though he was a timber worker, completed thirty days. The daughter spent most of her farming time on her husband's farms.

The actual contribution of different relatives varied also according to the maturity of the farms (Table 4.8). Thus the total work-load of wives was greater and hence more critical for farmers with younger farms. Much of the additional work-load of farmers with older farms was completed by hired labourers working on a permanent basis, though these farmers were not the heaviest users of hired labour.

TABLE 4.8 Contribution of labour to work on farms at Dominase, June 1971-May 1972

	No bearing farms at Dominase %	Bearing farms at Dominase[a] %
Male farmer	43.6	16.9
Offspring	1.0	3.6
Spouse	32.4	20.5
Female ma rikin	1.9	1.3
Male matrikin	2.2	9.3
Other farmers	1.4	9.7
Casual hired labour	17.5	12.3
Permanent hired labour	-	26.4
Total	100.0	100.0
Number of hours	7,630	23,815

[a]Excludes one farm where data for young and new farms were combined.

Note: Includes only farms where the owner was also the on-site manager. All the farms were owned by men.

Labour was hired at some time by all the farmers. Akosua Korantema, because of being absent and having no relatives to assist her, relied most on hired workers, followed by Kwame Asante's son and Adjoa Owusuwa. In Adjoa Owusuwa's case, since her farms were young and comparatively small, she relied on casual rather than permanent labour, whereas Kwame Asante's son and Akosua Korantema made more use of labour hired on a permanent basis. Omitting farms where owners themselves were absent, hired casual labour completed just over 40 per cent of the work on the women's farms, compared with 14 per cent on the men's, and even including the work done by the permanent hired workers this disparity in the use of labour between men and women remains. Among the men it was those with the younger holdings who relied most on casual labour and they, like their female counterparts, had therefore to meet relatively heavy immediate cash demands. In contrast, those with older holdings and a larger cash income were more able to rely on labour paid on the basis of output at the end of the cocoa season.

The various members of the labour force did not divide their labour similarly between the new, young and bearing farms (Table 4.9a and b). On average, wives spent more of their farm hours on the new and less on the young and bearing farms than their husbands. There were, however, two cases where wives worked more hours on bearing farms: Mr Mensah's three wives and Kofi Owusu's son's wife. In both instances the expansion of these farms was not the main feature of their farming programmes. Offspring spent even less time than wives on mature farms whereas male matrikin spent more of their time on these. This difference in the use of labour is more pronounced when differences in the ages of farms owned are considered. Among farmers with younger holdings only the male owners themselves divided their farming time fairly evenly between the young and new farms. Everyone else but the casual labourers was much more likely to work on the new farms. Hence although the total demand for labour was greater on the new farms, it was on the young farms that casual workers were more likely to be used.

TABLE 4.9a Time budgeting by members of the labour force on farms owned by men

	New %	Young %	Bearing %	Total %
Male farmer	45.5	31.6	22.9	100.0
Matrikin	19.4	46.5	34.1	100.0
Offspring	27.3	62.0	10.7	100.0
Wives	53.3	28.0	18.7	100.0
Matrikin	62.8	28.4	8.8	100.0
Other farmers	4.3	2.1	93.6	100.0
Casual labour	49.3	33.2	17.5	100.0
Permanent hired labour	6.1	1.6	92.3	100.0

In contrast, farmers with older holdings concentrated on their bearing farms, while male matrikin spent more time on the young farms and the women concentrated on the new farms. Sons, followed

TABLE 4.9b Time budgeting by members of the labour force between farms owned by men

	New %	Young %	Bearing %	Total %
No bearing farms at Dominase:				
Male farmer	52.2	47.8		100.0
Offspring	76.6	23.4		100.0
Wives	71.7	28.3		100.0
Female matrikin	81.6	18.4		100.0
Male matrikin	74.1	25.9		100.0
Other farmers	-	100.0		100.0
Casual labour	32.7	67.3		100.0
Bearing farms at Dominase:				
Male farmer	39.9	18.2	41.9	100.0
Male kin	15.4	48.0	36.6	100.0
Sons	23.0	65.4	11.6	100.0
Wives	44.0	27.8	28.2	100.0
Female kin	54.1	33.0	12.9	100.0
Other farmers	0.1	2.2	97.7	100.0
Casual labour	56.9	17.7	25.4	100.0
Permanent hired labour	6.1	1.6	92.3	100.0

Note: Differences in actual totals from previous publications are the result of changes in the numbers of farms to which the data refer. This table only refers to farms where the owner was working at Dominase and to farms owned by men.

by female matrikin and wives, spent the smallest proportion of their working hours on bearing farms.

The sexual division of labour on holdings reflects the different types of work to be done. As already observed, 25 per cent of the work on the new farms was connected with food production, including the major shade crop plantain, compared with only 5 per cent on young farms and a negligible amount on bearing farms. Using a slightly larger sample of farmers working on Dominase land and including both Akan and non-Akan farmers while combining data for young and old holdings, women were in general found to be more responsible for completing the work of planting and harvesting food crops than men (Table 4.10). Men, including the hired labourers, completed more of the work of felling, planting cocoa and maintenance other than weeding.

TABLE 4.10 Allocation of labour between tasks[a]

	Male farmer	Male relative	Wives	Female relatives	Hired/casual labour[b]	Other farmers	Care-takers	Annual labour
New farms:								
Clearing	8.5	-	-	-	91.5	-	-	-
Felling	33.1	3.9	5.6	-	57.4	-	-	-
Burning/Apam	32.3	4.0	32.2	-	22.0	-	9.5	-
Planting cocoa	46.9	8.6	30.5	1.0	3.7	-	6.6	2.7
Planting plantain	15.9	2.2	64.1	4.9	0.8	-	8.8	3.3
Planting other food crops	22.4	7.8	49.9	6.6	13.0	-	1.8	1.5
Harvesting food	19.9	4.0	50.0	19.0	1.8	-	-	5.3
Weeding	19.9	7.2	27.9	6.5	27.1	-	4.5	6.8
Making traps	52.6	15.6	-	-	31.6	-	-	-
Young farms:								
Planting cocoa	24.3	15.2	39.1	1.3	20.1	-	-	-
Planting plantain	-	-	100.0	-	-	-	-	-
Planting other food crops	44.6	-	49.0	-	6.4	-	-	-
Harvesting food	23.3	8.4	42.2	-	26.1	-	-	-
Weeding	23.9	3.2	14.3	0.4	57.9	-	0.3	-
Spraying	46.4	26.8	26.8	-	-	-	-	-
Other maintenance	100.0	-	-	-	-	-	-	-
Harvesting cocoa[c]	29.5	19.6	32.9	-	-	18.0	-	-

Bearing farms:								
Planting food	62.7	12.7	22.2	2.5	-	-	-	-
Harvesting food	7.8	4.0	86.0	-	2.3	-	-	-
Weeding	6.6	6.5	11.2	-	24.5	0.6	50.5	-
Other maintenance	59.3	8.6	18.1	-	2.9	-	14.0	-
Harvesting cocoa	10.2	5.8	12.2	1.2	-	37.2	33.0	-
Drying cocoa/ carrying	9.0	13.8	17.9	1.0	0.4	1.2	56.7	-

[a] Farms owned by thirteen Akan and two non-Akan male farmers only.

[b] Includes labourers hired on a daily basis and those hired on contract.

[c] Includes picking, collecting and breaking of pods.

Source: Okali (1975), p. 49.

One farmer differed from the other fourteen, relying heavily on hired workers to complete tasks connected with food crops on young and new farms, but this man, Kwadwo Kusi, planted food crops for sale. He, unlike any other farmer on any other single farm, did more work connected with food crop production than either of his wives or his son.

The type of work that women do on bearing farms is more restricted than that of men. The two most expensive tasks in terms of time are harvesting and weeding. Harvesting includes the picking of pods from the trees, collecting the pods into heaps, and breaking them to extract the beans. Both the actual picking and breaking is completed by men; farmers reported that women were unable to pick the pods from the trees.

In general, the incidence of task sharing between the sexes was high, especially where the work was time-consuming. Hence, both men and women spent much of their total farming time weeding even if they also specialised in other tasks, and although men were more concerned with work directly pertaining to the cocoa, all but one wife, Mr Ahinkurah's, assisted with cocoa planting.

Overall, the view that male farmers rely heavily on their wives for labour is confirmed by the farm management data from Dominase and indeed some farmers expressed the view that it would be impossible for them to start a cocoa farm without a wife. Thus when Kwame Asante's son was given land he married in the same year. Nevertheless, information collected from the farmers who were extending rather than starting new holdings at Dominase suggested that wives played a less significant role in land development, largely because when the farmers first started farming independently in their home towns, they were not married.

In this situation, when they might still have been assisting their fathers, it was their mothers who provided the labour to plant their first farms. Where they worked with mother's brothers rather than fathers, they would be responsible for their property development. Certainly at Dominase, these same men were relying heavily on their wives, particularly on the new farms where food crops were important.

Of interest are the two sets of wives who did more work on the bearing rather than the non-bearing farms. Mr Mensah had two bearing farms at Dominase, one of which had been handed to caretakers, while he cared for the other himself. The three wives had been promised a part share of this latter farm, which was still comparatively young. Mr Mensah was in fact little concerned with the expansion of new farms at Dominase and was himself preparing to leave the site for home to start a new farm there. The work on his small new farm started in 1972 was completed almost entirely by the junior wife. Similarly, Mr Owusu's son was caretaking bearing farms and had no new farms of his own. He did in fact later send his wife home to plant food crops while he stayed behind to look after the farms at Dominase.

Although there were not many adult children working on the farms at Dominase and they were exceeded in number by matrikin, Kwabena Danso's daughter and Kwame Asante's son completed more work for their fathers than any of the assistants, other than wives. Kwame

Asante's son also travelled to oversee some of the other farms owned by his father but this work is not included in the farm management data presented here. Mr Kusi, unlike Mr Mensah who also had numerous adult children, relied entirely on offspring and wives for assistance. Nevertheless, like the wives, offspring spent comparatively more of their time on the young and new farms.

Mr Danso was the only farmer who received much assistance in terms of total hours of work from sister's sons but this arrangement was not really satisfactory and was in a continuous state of flux. Mr Kusi had tried to work with matrikin when he first went to Dominase but failed, and Mr Poku was also not having much success, his mother's sister's sons being reluctant to stay with him. The most satisfactory arrangement was that of Mr Mensah who gave his matrikinsman considerable control over his farms and engaged him in other business activities.

Persons with only young farms at Dominase, and therefore including women, were the most isolated with respect to receiving labour from relatives and depended most on hired casual labour although the men were continuing to draw on an income from another source.

Although wives did invest their time heavily in their husbands' farms, a number were also engaged in their own separate non-farming business activities and this information is basic for understanding their economic relationship with their spouses. Three wives had separate trading interests. Kweku Amoa's wife, who travelled with her husband to caretake farms elsewhere, had a trading concern started with £18 from her husband which she repaid after two years. Her business was small, and involved little travelling to purchase items and also little time for selling - since customers came to her compound. Mr Okai's wife, a citizen, made pomade to sell and, of the three women, spent the most time on this separate concern of hers - fifty-two days over the year - although she had not relied on her husband for money with which to start it. Mr Okai said that he had intended to give his wife money to trade properly but a building that he had put up for storing cocoa beans took all his money. Mr Mensah's junior wife traded in fish that she purchased in her home town to sell both in her own compound and at the market. The two senior wives had their own food farms at home and they sold produce from these. The most senior, who was in her late forties and had fourteen children, was able to assist one of her brothers at college with ₵20 and another with ₵30 for marrying. She also bought school uniforms for her children. Finally Mr Ahinkurah's wife, who received annually proceeds from a bearing farm shared between herself and her siblings, also had an independent source of income. With this money she hired labourers to clear her own farm at Dominase and had also been able to loan money to a son.

Nine wives had no entirely separate economic interests of their own. Among their husbands, Mr Obese, Mr Ayesi and the son of Mr Owusu were all still trying to establish their own first farms and relied on other sources of income for doing this. Mr Obese worked as a carpenter while his wife worked odd days as a hired labourer, Mr Ayesi travelled to caretake a bearing farm and the son of Mr Owusu was caretaking for his father's heir. Unlike Mr Okai's local wife, their wives had no resources of their own, while at the same time they could expect little assistance from their husbands. Mr Okai had, in contrast, even received some assistance from his affines.

Mr Ayim and Mr Danso differed from the others in that they did receive a fairly substantial income from their cocoa farms even though Mr Danso was still being assisted by his mother's brother. Neither had provided money for their wives to start any business or farm independently. One of the issues over which Mr Danso quarrelled with his senior wife before she finally left was the lack of her own supply of money while he was preparing to take another wife. Overall, however, women with co-wives spent more time away from Dominase and hence had more time to spend on their separate activities.

MULTIPLE INTERESTS IN FARMS

The migrant cocoa farmer working in frontier areas has frequently been cited as an independent operator, free from the need to rely on customary kinship relationships for his production. However, these reports of citizen and stranger farmers on their pattern of cocoa farm investment, and details of actual labour used on farms over twelve months, demonstrated that these relationships are still important - and indeed in a number of cases made the migration possible. Thus as Hill (1963) concludes from her studies of the Akwapim cocoa farmers, the migratory process derives much of its strength and impetus from the fact that it is firmly based on traditional organisation. The case of Mr Ahinkurah, the citizen farmer at Dominase, was particularly interesting, therefore, since he among the men appeared to be operating most independently on stool land but outside his home town. Notably, among all the fifteen farmers, Akosua Korantema, the professional woman who had hired two annual labourers, was the most independent in this sense.

Although ties with matrikin were important for both citizen and stranger farmers, a significant feature of the details of sources of farms from Akokoaso and Dominase was the value of ties with matrikin, fathers, and even, in some situations, affines - as in the case of Mr Obese at Dominase - for acquiring land or farms.

Again, supporting the information on production units in Chapter 3, wives and offspring were contributing substantially to their husbands' and fathers' cocoa farm development at Dominase by providing labour. That this was the pattern for citizen farmers at Akokoaso was suggested briefly by a reference to Beckett's earlier work (Beckett, 1947). The few male farmers at Dominase who had tried to work closely with sister's sons had not had much success, with one exception. In the discussion of the Akan in Chapter 2, the ambiguity of the relationship between men and their sister's sons was mentioned; enmity arising from the latter's status as the farmer's potential heir may make relationships difficult to sustain. Nevertheless, a further explanation of the relationship between a man and his potential heir has been presented by Okali and Kotey (1971) using different data from Akokoaso. They point out that doubt over the actual heir to be appointed makes the practice of depending on mother's brothers economically precarious for any potential successor. Hence the most satisfactory relationship was that of

Mr Mensah who had already placed his potential heir in a position of authority and given him land to establish on his own. It is also interesting to note that brothers did not feature significantly as sources of labour although Mr Owusu, Mr Mensah, Mr Ayim and Mr Okai had each worked side by side with a brother at Dominase. This situation might again be explained by the fact that brothers were even closer to inheritance than sisters' sons. In contrast, the only two farm owners from patrilineal communities included in the farm management survey at Dominase were both assisted by younger brothers on a permanent basis. Among the fifteen Akan farmers, only Kofi Okai received help in the form of labour from a brother, in this case an older brother who was himself working independently.

The insignificance of matrikin among the permanent labour force working on the Dominase farms is consistent with the practice of attempting to separate the potentially conflicting ties of marriage, descent and parenthood. Kwabena Danso and Mr Owusu before he died were the only persons who tried to work using all sources of labour at the same time. In Mr Danso's case, his child was a daughter and Mr Owusu died before it was possible to see how the work was shared.

Labour for which immediate cash payment does not have to be made - principally that of wives and offspring - was particularly valuable to farmers just starting their cocoa holdings. Such a farmer, according to the law of diminishing marginal returns, expects the returns to his additional outgoings to be greater than those of a farmer expanding existing holdings. Nevertheless, the wealthier farmers at Dominase continued to receive assistance from their wives: although Mr Mensah's three wives each travelled frequently, there was always one at the farm site.

The concentration by wives on work on the new and young farms supports the view that they are aware that they are not working on a joint economic concern. Wives were expecting eventually to establish their own separate economic concerns and those who had been able to had done so. The female citizens were in an advantageous position in this respect since both had some separate sources of finance, while women who had co-wives appeared to have more freedom of movement than their counterparts with none. This pattern over time is consistent with the findings of Okali and Mabey (1975) in Ashanti that, as they age, men rely less on their wives and offspring for assistance on cocoa farms. At Dominase, Adjoa Owusuwa did no farm work for her husband over the twelve-month survey period, and Mr Mensah's two senior wives were each growing food crops in their home towns and spent more time away from Dominase than any of the other wives. Mr Mensah himself was preparing to leave Dominase since he had no more new land to clear. Women were responsible for much of the food production on the young farms, and were thus continuing in the role of food producers as at Akokoaso. Since as strangers their cultivation rights were restricted, they were unable to establish themselves even as subsistence producers on their own since in this capacity they would be unable to pay for the land. They therefore continued in the only way possible, on their husbands' farms.

The contrasting position of husbands and male matrikin who spent more of their farming time on the young and bearing farms supports the view that it is potentially a corporate concern that is being established.

While this division of labour exists and can be partly explained by the presence of food crops and inheritance rights, wives and offspring do complete other work, particularly weeding, which is the concern of everyone. It is possible to conceive that they may regard weeding as pertaining to the food crops, but nevertheless they are thereby assisting with the cocoa production. To explain this contribution of wives and offspring solely in terms of affective ties, doing things because one likes to, and the relationship between a man and his sister's sons in terms of enmity is inadequate, and this subject is followed more closely in Chapter 5. Since it is argued that wives do expect to operate independently in economic affairs, their continued presence as they age in circumstances where their spouses do not appear to be short of cash, and yet have not assisted them to work independently, needs to be explained. Thus how the various investors view their contributions, the security of their claims in view of potentially conflicting rights in farms, and how these claims are satisfied is the theme of the next chapter.

Chapter 5

Returns to investment

Persons who assist in farm development are likely to consider that they have thereby acquired certain rights in the property concerned, that is, in economic language, that they will get some return for their investment. Whether these assumed rights are considered binding, or merely hoped for, is significant for interpreting farm investment patterns but also for looking at the way in which returns are distributed. By looking at the dynamics of cocoa farm management in Chapter 4 it was demonstrated that although male farmers did rely on their wives, offspring and matrikin, the roles that each performed varied and thus, it is argued, their expectations will also vary. It will be seen however that the actual distribution of returns, regardless of expectations, cannot be explained solely by reference to specific investments in particular farms; this is basically because cocoa farming is not an isolated economic activity and farms are just one item in exchanges between individuals or groups.

Returns may be visible in the form of cash, food crops from young cocoa farms, land or other assistance with the establishment of separate properties and include ultimately the transfer of ownership of the farm itself following the death of the owner. The question of returns is therefore complicated. This complexity is further enhanced by the fact that reciprocation for assistance may not be immediate, especially where cash, farms or land are involved since cocoa farms are not fully mature until at least ten years after planting. Cocoa farmers are therefore involved in a long-term investment programme and this fact is even more significant among stranger farmers who pay for cultivation rights, and migrants as a whole, who are subject to various cash constraints when working in areas away from home towns. Since returns may not reflect inputs in farms but may rather be related to other services received or to other obligations of the farmers involved, it is at this point that cocoa farming is placed within the context of the total rights and obligations of the actors involved. This second aspect of production is pursued firstly by examining the expectations of those who have invested in the Dominase farms, and the way in which the farm owners were attempting to meet these. Conflicts or strains arising from unfulfilled expectations obviously did arise and these are discussed and subsequently examined using records of cases that have appeared in the civil courts. Finally a number of the findings are supported by reference to a different population of farmers in Ashanti.

RETURNS TO WIVES

Schneider (1974a), referring to the African subsistence producer, writes that women are a critical factor of production acting partly as capital (producing children) and partly as labour (producing crops) and there is no other significant labour (p. 221). In Ghana, hired labour is used significantly in the cocoa industry, particularly on bearing farms, but, as demonstrated in Chapters 3 and 4, relatives may still contribute substantially to work on farms, especially wives on their husbands' farms. Wives were found to be particularly important at Dominase where they were less likely to be operating independently than they would in their home towns, even in the separate production of food crops. Farmers with younger holdings received little assistance from relatives other than wives.

Since the new and young cocoa farms were the principal source of food crops at Dominase, the women concentrated their labour on these and the food crops were recognised at least in part as belonging to the wives - although the amount of control that each wife exercised over these varied.

Food crops are the only source of income from young cocoa farms and estimates of returns indicate that it can be considerable, especially that income deriving from the plantain and cocoyam (Rourke, 1974; Okali, 1975). However, not all farmers spent much time planting food crops and this seemed to be correlated with the distance of the farm from the market. Kwadwo Obese, whose farm was the most distant and whose returns were also small, spent the least time. Kwadwo Kusi, who was farming close to the camp site, planted yam for sale and even hired additional labour to complete the work involved.

Where the production unit consumed all or much of the food produced, which was the case with most of the farmers with younger groups of farms that were also small, there was no question about the sharing of food crops among assistants. Where possible sales were involved the rights of wives were clearly defined. At one extreme were the wives of Kweku Amoa, Mr Ahinkurah and Kwadwo Kusi, each of whom had comparatively free access to the food crops from the young farms.

> Kweku Amoa is Amma's second husband. They married about 10 years ago at a time when Kweku had just started his work at Dominase with money he had acquired from caretaking a bearing farm. She is now about 40, childless, and for the last two years has lived almost alone at Dominase itself whereas previously both she and her husband would stay for only brief periods. Amma's co-wife lives almost permanently at the site of the old farm in another locality altogether. Although both Amma and her husband still travel to the site of the old farm during harvest

time, Kweku was absent from Dominase 244 days compared with Amma's 123 during the survey year. Kweku is the youngest of the farmers with bearing cocoa at Dominase and has the smallest bearing acreage. Since his returns to land and labour were comparatively low, the income from this farm was the smallest of all those bearing, such that his caretaker received half share of the annual crop in compensation. Kweku depends mainly on the income he earns as caretaker of a mature farm elsewhere. Although Amma supervises the work at Dominase, she does not hire labour during her husband's absence. She is permitted to sell the foodstuffs from the young farms which would seem to be explained to a large extent by the fact that she has much of the responsibility for them. Kweku assisted only with the plantain which provides essential shade for the young cocoa, but even here Amma did most of the work.

Mr Ahinkurah, the 65-year-old citizen farmer, and Sefoa, his wife from the same town, have now been married for about 20 years and for each of them this was their third marriage. They have seven children together, three of whom live at Mim town and to whom they send both money and food crops from the young cocoa farms, which are their only source of food crops. Mr Ahinkurah is the only one of the older residents who has been unsuccessful in establishing his cocoa at Dominase and, as recorded earlier, he complained of elephants when he first arrived at Dominase and hence neglected the farm for a number of years. During the survey year Sefoa was very sick and since there was little cash to hire labour, the new farms were again neglected. Like Kweku Amoa's wife, Sefoa says that she can sell whatever she wants from the farms and does not need to tell her husband. From the labour data, only Sefoa spent time on the food crops during the year while her husband planted the cocoa. In actual fact they consume most of what they produce because their children are still young and Mr Ahinkurah is one of the few farmers who has stated openly that the reason why he plants a new cocoa farm every year, even though that land which is already planted is not doing well, is because he needs the food crops.

In cases involving more than one wife, the young farms were divided between them. The two wives of Kwadwo Kusi also sell food crops from the young and new farms; these are quite considerable since Kwadwo has the largest young farms (28 acres) and the family's immediate consumption needs are not great.

Although Mr Kusi has twenty-one children, most of them are grown and only one, a married son, resides in the same compound with him at Dominase, accompanied by his wife and young son. Mr Kusi's other children live elsewhere. Mr Kusi's caretakers who work on this farm, and their wives and children, also reside in the same compound, but they harvest their food crops from the bearing farm which they are caretaking. Kwadwo himself is also interested in the food crops and indeed when visiting his new farm for the first time he referred to it as a yam rather than a cocoa farm. Nevertheless, although his main interest lies in the yams and these are only sold by him, he also assists with planting plantain and other food items which his wives are permitted to sell. Although Mr Kusi's bearing farm at Dominase gives a comparatively low return per acre, because of its size he derives the second largest cocoa income from it and overall, including the income from food crops and his bearing farm at home, Kwadwo is among the wealthiest farmers in the community as a whole.

At the other extreme were the wives of Alex Mensah, Kwame Ayim and Kwabena Danso, among whom, because there was more than one wife, the new farms were again divided for the purpose of planting and harvesting certain food crops. Here, however, their husbands received the money from any sales of corn, cocoyam and plantain even though each was already a comparatively successful cocoa farmer, not only within the group of fifteen farmers being discussed here but within the community as a whole. All three had bearing farms that, on the basis of their inputs and returns, placed them among those achieving the best returns, and Kwame Ayim had the largest cocoa income from his Dominase farms of all those with bearing farms included in the survey. Akosua Addae, his senior wife, describes their own arrangements.

> When asked about the food crops on her husband's farms, Akosua says that Kwame permits them to take and sell them and keep the money if they can weed throughout the farms the whole time. If not, they must give him the money which he would use to hire labourers. Akosua says she cannot do the weeding so she gives him the money. For the past two years he has told them not to sell anything because there are too many people around him, although he has only four children at Dominase and his two wives. However, if they plant okra, pepper and tomato they can sell but if the husband plants they have to give him the money.

As Akosua's account suggests, the wives did plant vegetables while at the same time they also assisted with the plantain and other food items. The importance of even these smaller food crops consisting of vegetables was demonstrated by other women at Dominase. Kwame Ayim's brother's wife, also one of two wives, said that the young farm was for all. Thus both she and the co-wife were given equal shares of the husband's new farm to plant food crops. On a farm visit, accompanied by her co-wife's mother and her husband's eldest son, she complained that the son had shown the old woman her own pepper to pick; she was complaining bitterly.

Alex Mensah's three wives all accounted to him for the sales of plantain and cocoyam from his farms and the senior wife, talking of her husband's new farm in their home town, described how it was divided among them for planting food crops.

The growing of food crops is an essential part of the farming programme and once the new cocoa farms are no longer sufficient for consumption needs alternative arrangements are made. Hence Kofi Owusu's son sent his wife home towards the end of the survey with money to hire labour to clear a food farm because he had no land for planting a new farm at Dominase. Alex Mensah's two senior wives were each working for a large part of the year on their food farms at home where all their children lived.

Food crops are not usually mentioned as being part of the returns to women but land or farms are. Indeed it is the incidence of men giving land or parts of farms to wives and offspring that has led observers to comment on changes in relationships between spouses and offspring arising from cocoa farming. In many cases these gifts are being made for assistance received in the past in the development of cocoa lands. Although the continued involvement of women in food production at Dominase has been emphasised, the labour data also indicated that they did other jobs. It was argued that even if this work could be viewed as pertaining to the food crops, the wives were indirectly assisting with the cocoa. Nevertheless, the participation of the women, including wives, decreased as the farm aged, while that of their husbands and male matrikin increased. The women still harvested the food crops and, apart from weeding and assisting with cocoa harvesting by collecting the pods into heaps, they did other work, such as carrying water to mix with insecticide for spraying. Generally, however, in spite of the women's continued participation, the mature farms were considered to belong to the men, as was confirmed one day when Kwame Ayim's bearing farm was visited during his absence. Many neighbouring farmers had gathered to break Mr Ayim's cocoa and Akosua, his senior wife, went very late to see if all was well. On her arrival at the farm, the farmers were preparing to leave, having finished the work and eaten food prepared by the caretaker's wives. They had also been promised food crops from the farm which they were to harvest themselves. Akosua went to a section promised to her by her husband to harvest food for herself but was followed by some of the cocoa breakers. Akosua grew very angry, saying that she did not see why they should follow her since they had not been working for her but rather for the caretakers, and that they could see that she had not harvested much. She knew that it could lead to trouble in her own compound and said that that was why she had been reluctant to go to her husband's farm that day. Like Akosua, none of the wives assumed that they had established a joint concern with their husbands in that both had equal rights in it, although they did expect some compensation other than the food crops, possibly even a fraction of the established farm.

For the farmers who were just beginning to establish themselves independently, it was a period of investment. Among these farmers were Yaw Ayisi, Kofi Okai, Kwadwo Obese and Kweku Amoa and the deceased Kofi Owusu's son, who had hardly started to work independently. None of these men mentioned having made any arrangement for establishing farms on behalf of their wives or their children although in each case in addition to providing labour, wives were also contributing financially to domestic needs, either by trading or by other means. Each would have been hard pressed to have established any additional farm at the time without financial assistance and all relied heavily on incomes from other sources to make their work at Dominase possible. In addition, wives, by completing the work on the new farms, were saving half of the labour costs. Kweku Amoa did loan his wife money to trade which she repaid, and Kofi Okai did say that he had wanted to do the same but found he would have been unable to meet all his expenses at the same time. However, such financial arrangements were regarded in a totally different way from the gift of farms, or land to farm where no question was raised about returning the initial investment which the husband himself might have made. This was so even in the case of Adjoa Owusuwa who was provided with land comparatively soon after her marriage and certainly not in return for help on farms.

In contrast to the group of farmers with younger holdings, among the others, all but Kweku Amoa had at least stated their intention of making some separate provision for their wives and offspring either by providing land, farms or labour. Nevertheless this was many years after the husbands established their own first farms. For the most part, they were not considering any entirely separate property and arrangements were, to say the least, often vague.

Five of the sixteen wives had already started working on separate farms - including Adjoa Owusuwa who spent all her farming time on them, Alex Mensah's three wives, and Mr Ahinkurah's wife. Mr Ahinkurah was the only man who was reported to be using his own labour. Alex Mensah provided money for labour to be hired. It was not, however, only the men who were investing in these separate properties. Mr Ahinkurah's wife said that she used part of her share of the proceeds of a bearing farm for hiring labour to clear her land even though her husband was assisting with labour.

Other women had been promised parts of established farms but these were not being operated as distinct units; these women included the wives of Kwame Ayim, Kwabena Danso and Alex Mensah. Kwabena Danso's arrangements were the least distinct. Mr Danso claimed that he made a larger farm the year he arrived at Dominase which was to be shared between his two wives, but the senior, dissatisfied with her position, left before any transfer was finalised. Mr Poku also claimed that he had made provision for his wife but no specific area was indicated.

These provisions were being made for wives when the farmers were themselves well established. Mr Mensah's senior wife had been married to him for twenty-four years. She was joined by the second wife after six years and the third almost eighteen years after her own marriage. Mr Ahinkurah's wife, Sefoa, was starting her farm eleven years after first coming to Dominase and they had probably been married almost sixteen years. She said in her interview that she had never worked apart from her husband before. Most of the women had been married a number of years even if this was not their only marriage and, except Mr Mensah's junior wife and Adjoa Owusuwa, each had assisted with the development of the holding at Dominase from the time when it was first started. Some farmers obviously make preparations late as was demonstrated by the case of Kofi Owusu. Kofi Owusu was in the process of purchasing a separate plot for his junior wife just before he died. Fortunately for her the heir finalised this arrangement.

The size of the farms involved was comparatively small, although the women did not voice dissatisfaction and there was in any case no agreement about how much land or farm a woman might expect to have. It was not possible in all cases to measure, partly because the farmers were themselves sometimes vague, but the young farm for Mr Mensah's three wives was 2.2 acres, and even if they take over the whole of the young Amazon bearing farm - which is unlikely since Mr Mensah did not even wish to discuss the matter - only an area of 4 acres is involved. Kwame Ayim had given to each of his two wives 2 acres from his 37 bearing acres. Again Adjoa Owusuwa probably had one of the largest acreages with three young farms covering 4 acres. Assuming a production of ten loads to an acre, which is high in view of the average production in Ghana as a whole, at the current price of ¢16.00 per load, an acre would give a gross income of ¢160. One third of this may be paid to caretakers leaving approximately ¢100 per acre net return. Using the same estimates of building costs mentioned earlier, it would be possible to build a house, for instance, with these returns assuming one had other sources of income for maintenance.

The final, and probably the most important point about all the reported provisions, was that none of the women had finalised any of the customary transfer arrangements for either the land or parts of farms indicated. This included Adjoa Owusuwa who had been operating independently for three years and the three wives of Mr Mensah. Akosua Addae, the senior wife of Mr Ayim, said that she was ready to take over the bearing section the year following the survey and would tell her elder sister to make arrangements. Akosua planned to give her part to a caretaker and her husband said that she could use the proceeds for building a house for her children in her home town. This delay, as Akosua herself reported, was related partly to the fact that the husbands were bearing part of the establishment costs which they would probably no longer be prepared to do once the transfer was complete. However, I suggest it is also linked with the problem of what happens when an exchange is effected, a woman having received some compensation for her assistance. Certainly if it is not effected in time, a woman may terminate the relationship by divorce - as probably will finally occur in the case of Mr Danso's wife who left dissatisfied. Notably, it was her daughter who contributed substantially to the work on Mr Danso's new and young farms. The wife, however, considered that her case was even deteriorating after fifteen years of marriage since her husband was preparing to take a third wife. The information on residence and production units presented in Chapter 3 suggested that in any case women were likely to be unmarried when they were cocoa farming and data from Okali and Mabey (1975) also show that as they get older Ashanti men no longer rely on their wives for labour.

It has been suggested that wives are being given land or farms on behalf of their children, and vice versa; this argument is again followed more closely in the subsequent analysis of disputes in court. Kwadwo Kusi appeared to be operating in both ways as will be discussed in the next section. A number of the women had grown children who had been educated by their fathers and this could be regarded as an alternative to providing them with a trade or business. This was so in the case of Mr Mensah, but even he was also making some separate arrangements for their mothers, suggesting that wives can receive in their own right. However, Adjoa Owusuwa had received farms but had not herself invested in those of her husband. At the end of the survey she had three children, the oldest six years of age, and since her husband had many offspring, Adjoa being his sixth wife, it is possible that he was considering the young children rather than Adjoa herself when giving her land for separate farms.

RETURNS TO OFFSPRING

Adult offspring who have assisted their fathers on farms are also likely to expect some return. Their contribution to farm development at Dominase, like that of their mothers, was in the form of labour and again was restricted mainly to the younger farms. At Akokoaso the analysis of production units indicated that few adult offspring were assisting their parents and at Dominase, among the fifteen cases, they were exceeded in number by matrikin. Nevertheless where offspring did assist on a permanent basis, their contribution was relatively substantial. Thus Kwame Asante's two elder sons were entirely responsible for the development of their father's property and Kwabena, who was resident at the time of the survey, had worked six years at the site. Mr Asante's sons were the only ones among the adult offspring who actually received a separate piece of land before the survey finished. Their father had already established three farms before reaching Dominase and therefore they were in a fortunate position.

Kwadwo Kusi was also relying on a married son at Dominase although he was present at the site most of the time, and his daughter was working on the bearing farms at home. The son's wife, who already had one child, did not work with him. Kwadwo claimed that he had offered part of the 27-acre young farm to all his twenty-one children to share, but he admitted that one of them would not care for the farm and then share with everyone else. Thus he was looking after the farm himself. His son assisting at Dominase was certainly not satisfied, one of his complaints being that his father had refused to pay for his secondary education, and he was preparing to return to his home town to plant cocoa on land provided by his mother's brother. Kwadwo, a comparatively wealthy man, had provided separate plots of land for his sister's daughter's son, and five sisters and their sons. Two other relatives had been given part of the land he was developing at Dominase. Only one of his children was being catered for by the provision of a separate plot and both Kwadwo and his junior wife, the mother of this child, travelled to a nearby site to do the work. As noted earlier, the position of caretaker is considered to be the best among the possible contractual arrangements for labourers, and Kwadwo, by reserving this work for a senior daughter and spouse, could be seen to have been caring for her needs separately. It would hardly have been possible for this exchange to have been anything other than direct since it involved both daughter and spouse who had no binding rights on Kwadwo as would lineage members. Thus Kwadwo's married son, although younger, was preparing to leave. Once his father had failed to provide for his future and an alternative was offered there was no question of his staying at Dominase. Kwabena Danso's unmarried daughter who left Dominase with her mother has already been mentioned.

The duty of a father with respect to his offspring is clearly stated by Fortes (1950), who writes that it is to feed, clothe, educate and later set them up in life. Bearing this in mind, offspring would seem to be in a more secure position than their mothers with respect to claims since, as Fortes points out, there can be no question of offspring being obliged to assist their fathers. Once they receive sufficient land and have the resources to develop it - which at Dominase appeared to include a wife - male offspring will work on their own as did Kwame Asante's first son. Nevertheless, offspring, like their mothers, are involved in a long-term investment programme and may be disappointed. Kofi Owusu's married son, who was thirty-five when his father died, had always worked with him. Before his father's death he not only worked at Dominase but also travelled to their home town to harvest his father's self-acquired bearing farm. The main development of Mr Owusu's holding was a 14-acre new section that was to have at least partly provided for his wives and children. The development of this farm was curtailed by his sudden death. The disappointment of his eldest son, who was given a 4-acre portion of the new farm, is reflected in his own comment on the situation: 'If you follow your father you are a fool for nothing'. Not only was the farm still young but it was neglected for some time following Mr Owusu's death and its division into various parts. His son was still therefore in a very dependent economic position but was retained by his father's heir as caretaker of the two bearing farms at Dominase for which he would receive a fixed share of the crop. Thus the heir was fulfilling his duties of caring for the economically dependent offspring of the deceased by entering into an exchange which, like that between Kwadwo Kusi and his daughter and son-in-law, was direct, immediate and fixed, and in which there seemed to be no question of either party being in a superior or inferior position.

Most of the farmers with adult sons had in fact educated them and they were not working as farmers. However, the fact that fathers may be working closely with sons on farms hardly seems to present a serious threat to the corporate rights of descent groups. Thus Mr Kusi, although he provided for his children, first made either land or parts of farms available for his matrikin. Mr Owusu's farms were divided among many, including his son and sister's son, both of whom had assisted him during his lifetime, and his heir, who had not.

RETURNS TO MATRIKIN

Two categories of matrikin who have invested in farms must be clearly distinguished, those who from the information might expect reciprocation and those who do not. In addition, when considering rights and obligations of matrikin we are looking both at individuals and the corporate group as a whole. Among the individuals are nephews working for their mothers' brothers while having no independent income of their own. Of the Dominase farmers, Mr Danso, Mr Mensah and Mr Owusu before his death were working with their sisters' sons on a permanent basis. Matrikin were also supervising work on bearing farms elsewhere but these were more senior kinsmen who themselves had farms, and for them there was no question of expecting a direct return for assistance given. Among this second group of matrikin are the mother's brothers of Mr Danso and Mr Ayim and a large number of temporary assistants who included mothers, sisters, a brother and sisters' sons. Most of the twelve male owners at Dominase had received assistance from this category of persons, who were in a position to give rather than to receive. In a number of instances this was in the form of contacts, money or land to make the venture possible in the first place. In the cases of Mr Poku and Mr Owusu, part of their financial backing came from the proceeds of farms that they had inherited and that were therefore lineage property. The position of this group of persons can only be understood if account is taken of the corporate nature of descent groups and the sense of obligation existing between members, doing things for one another because they must, particularly men for their sisters' sons. A good mother's brother is expected to help his sister's sons, thereby obliging the latter to reciprocate in the next generation either through their own sisters' sons or through other matrilineal dependants (Fortes, 1950). Returns are not always therefore related directly to inputs on farms, as was observed in the case of Mr Owusu's heir. Kwadwo Kusi, Kwesi Poku and Alex Mensah had each made gifts to matrikin of farms or land that could not be related directly to inputs. Mr Kusi purchased four pieces of land for the children of four sisters, and one for his eldest sister that was to have been for his own mother, who died before he was able to complete the project; Mr Poku had offered land to the adult offspring of his mother's sister. In Mr Kusi's case the only assistance he claimed to have received from matrikin was labour from a grandnephew when he first arrived at Dominase, whereas Mr Poku did rely financially on matrikin and used the proceeds of a family farm that he had inherited, although he had until then received little help from his grandnephews. Mr Mensah said that he had purchased land for a brother who had not worked for him.

It has already been mentioned that among the most unsatisfactory relationships at Dominase were those between a man and his sister's son. This was ascribed partly to the uncertainty of the latter's appointment as heir, since although sisters' sons inherit in accordance with seniority by age of their mothers, character is also considered and the heir must be approved by the lineage head and his elders. Thus Kofi Owusu's sister's son who was working on his farms did not inherit the property. If it is accepted that there are two types of transactions between matrikinsmen, direct and indirect, it is also possible to see insecurity increased by assistance being regarded as part of the whole series of exchanges. Thus the claims of sisters' sons may be merged with the rights of the corporate concern. Only the relationship between Mr Mensah and his sister's son, who was already benefiting directly, was satisfactory. It is possible therefore that sisters' sons feel even less economically secure than offspring.

The position of sisters' sons as recipients of assistance may also not be enviable since it incurs the obligation to reciprocate. This may explain the behaviour of Mr Poku's mother's sister's children who refused his offer of land for farm development, a direct exchange, although it does not satisfactorily explain the situation of Mr Ayim. Mr Ayim, whose mother's brother had purchased two tracts of land for him, expressed the view that if he accepted the second he would spend all his time establishing farms for matrikin. I have already argued that by satisfying a particular exchange, the relationship, if continued - as it obviously will be among matrikin - is also likely to change. Before the exchange is satisfied, either directly or indirectly, the recipient is placed in a subordinate position, whereas afterwards the relationship may involve friendliness and respect. Both Kwabena Danso and Kwame Ayim had received substantial assistance from their mothers' brothers. Kwabena Danso was himself however still unable to reciprocate either directly or indirectly. In this subordinate position he also found himself unable to give information on the development of the family farms as a whole and eventually cancelled an invitation to visit his home town and discuss these. Kwame Ayim, in contrast, had reached a point where he could buy his own land and no longer wished to be placed in a subordinate position. He therefore repaid the amount spent on the second piece of land. It is possible to view his relationship with his wives within the same context. Thus in contrast to Mr Danso, he had given a definite area of farm to his two wives, one of whom reported that she was preparing to finalise takeover arrangements. We can distinguish among the other farmers on the same basis. Mr Ayim compares with Mr Mensah, Mr Kusi and Mr Poku, each of whom had been able to make some provision for wives and offspring although arrangements were by no means finalised, while each had first provided for matrikinsmen.

The rights of the descent group as a corporate unit are ultimately established through inheritance. The sharing of farms following death and the subsequent care of the farm is the subject that first inspired the present study. The only property at Dominase that was divided during the survey was that of Kofi Owusu. Here, that part of the holding that was already established and yielding cocoa all went to the heir and included two inherited farms and two that Mr Owusu had acquired himself during his lifetime. The younger farms of 15 acres, where the oldest trees were two years old at the time of his death, and which still required considerable investment, were divided among his two wives, his own son, and his sister's son who had worked for him during his lifetime. The heir had never worked on any of the farms himself and had earlier even been in a position to offer assistance to Mr Owusu.

Although other farmers at Dominase had already gifted or arranged to give parts of farms to wives and offspring, overall the remaining acreage was still the larger proportion. Certainly earlier investigations at Akokoaso, using the same sample of farmers as Beckett (1947), demonstrated that the majority of the acreage of the ten holdings was inherited (Okali and Kotey, 1971) even though wives and children were reported by Beckett to have contributed substantially to the work-load. But, as with Dominase farmers, this occurred mostly when the farms were still very young and when they were still therefore the main source of food for consumption.

CONFLICTS IN COURT

Claims to rights in farms and the problem of meeting these can also be followed from records of cases filed in the civil courts. From the arguments presented, the basis and security of the various claims and the different situations that lead to conflict are highlighted. In addition, a number of issues not covered in the Dominase cases are also raised; these include in particular the question of divorce and ensuing claims and the problem of the management of corporate property.

Just over half of the records of disputes involving relatives covered parties related through marriage (Table 5.1). Cases in this category were significantly represented in the records taken from courts in the Brong Ahafo and Eastern Regions where usufructuary rights in farms have been purchased, suggesting that it is in these situations that the significance of marital ties is increased (Table 5.2). On the other hand, disputes between matrikin, comprising just less than half of the records, dominated those taken from courts located in Kumasi, which referred mostly to farms located within the Ashanti Region.

INTER-FAMILY DISPUTES

Conflicts between members of different descent groups largely concerned wives and offspring and the descent group of their deceased spouses and fathers. Among these, offspring appeared in almost half the cases and usually on their own behalf (Table 5.3). Wives were equally as likely to be appearing on their own as on their children's behalf.

CLAIMS OF OFFSPRING

One out of every two of the disputes concerning offspring of deceased persons arose out of gifts of land or farms made by their fathers, most frequently during their fathers' lifetimes, and not on claims of inheritance rights (Table 5.4). In making claims to gifts, only in four instances was reference made to services performed, including labour on farms, as in the case of Kwame Amponsah v. Yaw Barimah which first appeared at Kumasi High Court in 1974. Here, the son claimed that after he had helped his late father to clear a virgin forest seventeen years previously, he was given in return a portion of land to cultivate into a cocoa farm. Later, when his father became involved in a court case, the son offered to use the proceeds of the farm to help defray legal expenses and by the time his father died this debt had been repaid.

In only one dispute did offspring make reference to customary rights and here a son was claiming to be administrator of his father's estate and his only male relation at their place of residence. In reply to the plaintiff, who was also claiming the position of heir, the son averred that he was only a good friend of his father. Since he was not old enough at the time to administer all the properties, the plaintiff was permitted meanwhile to supervise on his behalf (Kwabena Kyereme v. Kwadwo Badu, Circuit Court, Sunyani, 1969).

In most instances, as far as can be seen from the records, claims of gifts are made without reference to any justification, litigants being more concerned to prove their claims in terms of the procedure of gift giving itself. Thus in the dispute between Akua Asabah v. Kwadjo Amoah and another, first heard on appeal at the Koforidua High Court in 1974, it was recorded simply that 'The defence in this

TABLE 5.1 Relationship between litigants in court cases

Plaintiff	Defendant: Matrikin of deceased	Wife/offspring of deceased	Son	Uterine sibling	Ex-spouse	Patrikin
Matrikin of deceased	49	20[b]				
Wife/offspring of deceased	23[a]					
Father			3			
Uterine sibling				9		
Ex-spouse					13	
Patrikin	1					4
N = 122						

[a] Includes two cases of wife divorced prior to death of spouse and one where wife supported by matrikin of spouse.

[b] Includes one case of wife divorced prior to death of spouse and one where wife supported by matrikin of spouse.

TABLE 5.2 Category of cases by court location

	Ashanti region	Brong Ahafo region	Eastern region	Accra	Number of cases
Intra-family dispute	16	27	12	3	58
Inter-family dispute	11	34	13	4	62
Intra- and inter-family dispute	-	1	1	-	2
N = 122					

Note: Details of years from which records are taken are given in Appendix 3.

TABLE 5.3 Relationship between litigants involved in inter-family disputes

Plaintiff	Defendant						
	Matrikin of deceased	Wife of deceased	Wife/offspring of deceased	Offspring of deceased	Ex-spouse	Son	Other
Matrikin of deceased		3	2	14[b]	1[c]		
Wife of deceased	7[a]						
Wife/offspring of deceased	8						
Offspring of deceased	8						
Ex-spouse					13[d]		
Father						3	
Other							5
N = 64							

[a]Includes two cases of wife divorced prior to spouse's death and one where wife was supported by spouse's matrikin.

[b]Includes one where wife was supported by father's matrikin.

[c]Of deceased.

[d]Includes one case of ex-husband as plaintiff. In all other cases, wife is plaintiff.

TABLE 5.4 Basis of claims of offspring against father's matrikin[a]

Claims	Litigants				
	Mothers and offspring	Offspring[b]	Daughter/s	Son/s	Number of cases
Gift inter vivos[c]	6	4	3	2	15
Last Will and Testament	-	2	-	2	4
Farms developed by deceased/wife and children	-	1	-	2	3
Gift of land for assistance	-	1	-	1	2
Permission to plant by father	1	1	-	-	2
Maintenance	1	-	-	1	2
Other	1	1	1	1	4
N = 32					

[a] In one instance claims of offspring were not recorded.

[b] Including both sons and daughters.

[c] Aseda given and gift made in public.

Note: Offspring may be appearing as prosecution or defence.

case is based on the will of the deceased whom the plaintiff succeeded. The property concerned is devised to them by their late father, the late ______________ under his Last Will and Testament.'

The court records show that even where a gift of land or farms has been made, the gift can be disputed (Table 5.5). Gifts were disputed on various grounds and frequently involved different stories of how farms came to be in the possession of the persons involved, as the following case illustrates.

> The plaintiffs' account
> The plaintiffs claimed that their father cultivated all his farms and gave them to his children, the plaintiffs, during his lifetime. The gifts were made in the presence of witnesses with the customary payment of £8.8s and two bottles of Schnapps having been made by the recipients. Their father further executed a will leaving his property to his children.
> The defendants' account
> The defendants, members of the father's maternal family, claimed on the other hand that all the items in dispute were their family property. One of the farms had been inherited by the deceased and could not therefore be given away, and the remaining three, as the plaintiffs knew, were pledged to repay funeral expenses incurred following their father's death. The children had made no claims of ownership following their father's death nor had they objected to the pledging of the farms. Finally, in his last will, the deceased had left all his properties to his heir to be held in trust for the family of the deceased. (Kofi Nyame and others v. Kofi Nyame Asiama and others, Kumasi High Court, 1967)

The most common claim by matrikin disputing gifts, as in the above instance, is that farms were already family property, having been inherited. This suggests that if such claims are true then the giving of gifts is not itself in dispute but rather the giving away of family properties. Certainly it is possible that offspring may be unaware of the actual history of farm development. The adult children of Alex Mensah at Dominase, for instance, claimed, on visiting their father's old farm in his home town, that they had never been there before and did not know the boundaries; they were also ignorant of a house built by their father for his mother.

The provision of inputs, including payments for land and the use of matrikin for labour were used in support of claims by families in only four instances, which is similar to the significance that is attributed to this kind of argument by offspring themselves. Possibly this is one of the most difficult arguments to sustain just because of the many sources of inputs in farms and the problem of providing evidence, especially when referring to incidents that occurred many years ago.

When offspring, but particularly sons, have assisted their fathers to establish farms, and later have looked after or even been given bearing farms, it may be claimed that in fact the offspring were operating merely as caretakers rather than having permanent rights in the farms. In the case of Kwame Amponsah v. Yaw Barimah, first heard at Kumasi High Court in 1974, although the son claimed

TABLE 5.5 Claims against offspring by father's matrikin[a]

Claims	Mother and offspring	Offspring	Daughters	Sons	Number of cases
Family/inherited[b] property	3	4	1	3	11
Source of inputs	–	2	–	2	4
Offspring only caretakers	–	2	–	1	3
Neglect by offspring/ no assistance	1	–	1	–	2
Part already gifted	1	1	–	–	2
Denial/rights of heir, etc.	3	1	2	3	9
N = 31					

[a]In two instances claims against offspring were not recorded.

[b]Either the land undeveloped or farms.

Note: Offspring may be appearing as prosecution or defence.

to have established the farm himself, the heir contended that the son was only allowed to take care of the said farm on an abusa basis (1) about eight years before his father's death. Since then the son had been permitted to continue to care for the farm on an abusa basis.

This particular type of argument by members of descent groups would seem to be supported where offspring claim that they have even used the proceeds of such properties to assist their fathers, as noted earlier in this case or where farms are used to defray funeral expenses incurred by his matrikin, as in four other disputes.

> In the dispute between Abena Nnuro and others v. Thomas Owusu, first heard at Sunyani High Court in 1972, offspring claimed that they received a cocoa farm from their father as a gift. The father's heir, his uterine brother, succeeded and held the property in trust for them and shared the proceeds between them. Later the children agreed that the proceeds of the farm should be used for paying their father's debts. Following the death of the first heir, the offspring further allowed the next heir to use part of the proceeds for building a house on a family plot, after which they claimed the farm. The defendant merely stated that no gift of a farm was made to the children but rather their father handed the farm to them to maintain.

Among these disputes three involved a ruling of a Christian church on the issue of the distribution of property following death. The following is a case where, contrary to our expectations, the church ruling led to a reallocation of property in favour of a man's heir.

> The Plaintiffs were the widow and children of the deceased who was the brother of the defendant. The widow had been married according to Presbyterian Canon Law. During his lifetime her spouse gave her the property in dispute: an iron bedstead, one shot gun and a cocoa farm. The defendant, the successor, refused to acknowledge these gifts and made claim to them. He alleged that the property of the deceased was shared between the plaintiff and himself in accordance with the Presbyterian system following which the property in dispute was given to him. Both, according to his statement, had been satisfied with the arbitration and had paid aseda to seal the award. (Madam Agnes Agyeiwaa and children v. Kwame Adu, Koforidua High Court, 1972)

Rarely are the offspring of deceased persons found litigating side by side with their father's matrikin but one dispute did involve the offspring and uterine sister of a man as plaintiffs, and his heir as defendant. The plaintiffs, however, were making independent claims. Thus the children were seeking maintenance from their father's estate whereas the sister was accusing her brother,

---

1 A caretaker arrangement whereby the produce is divided into three parts, one part going to the caretaker as payment for his services.

the heir, of wasting family properties and not maintaining his various nephews, including sons of a deceased sister (Paul Edward Nkrumah and others v. Kwabena Num, Sunyani High Court, 1972).

That offspring were only acting as caretakers rather than owners was the issue in all three suits involving fathers prosecuting sons: in the case of Martey Narh Kwaku v. Gabriel Kofi Kumah at the Koforidua Circuit Court in 1970, the father stated that some time in 1960 he employed his son to take charge of the farm in dispute, and to render account to him of the proceeds, which he did for only three years. The son contended that his father gave him the land in 1948, and he developed it into a farm. He also claimed that in 1963 when his father made his first claim of ownership, the matter went before arbitrators where it was decided that the land should be divided into two.

In one of these cases, the son, who was using the farm as security for a loan, admitted that he was only a caretaker receiving one-third of the proceeds, but said that he had thought he could liquidate the debt with his own returns. Since he had failed, the farm was being claimed by the creditors (Opanyin Kwadwo Waaye v. Kwame Dakwah and others, Circuit Court, Sunyani, 1971).

The frequency with which offspring appear in cases, with or without their mothers, supports the suggestion made earlier that they have more rights than their mothers, and that men more frequently make gifts to offspring than to wives.

CLAIMS OF WIVES

Suits involving relatives by marriage can be divided into two equal groups, those arising from conflicts of women with former husbands and those arising from conflicts of women with their late husband's matrikin. It is significant that over two-thirds of these disputes involve divorcees.

In both situations the most common conflicts are those arising from rights to gifts, either of land or farms (Table 5.6). In less than one in five of these disputes was a demand being made on behalf of offspring - as by Madam Afua Achiaa v. Madam Yaa Aboraa at the District Court, Goaso, in 1972.

> Afua, disputing with her deceased husband's matrikin, said that her late husband left ten children, of whom five were still at school. During their marriage she and her husband had worked jointly on cocoa farms and made akpateshie, (2) yet her husband's family had refused to give her anything, not even the one farm which he had prepared for the upkeep of the children.

In the next case a wife was claiming a gift of a farm from her former husband. Also of interest is the point made by the wife that the dispute over the farm led to the divorce.

---

2 Locally brewed gin.

TABLE 5.6 Claims of wives and divorcees

Claims	Divorcee v. spouse	Wife v. matrikin of spouse[a]	Divorcee v. matrikin of spouse[a]	Total
Gift to self for assistance	2	3	1	6
Gift and/or child maintenance	2	1	1	4
Maintenance for self	-	1	-	1
Gift of land only	2	1	-	3
Gift of farm/ no reason	1	1	-	2
Land not for spouse	3	-	1	4
Customary rights/ church ruling[b]	2	1	-	3
N = 23				

[a]Spouse deceased.

[b]Customary right referred to was Dormaa Customary law that states that where spouses work jointly each has a right to a share, or wife has a right to compensation following divorce without due cause. Church ruling refers to ruling of the Presbyterian Church.

Note: Parties may be appearing as prosecution or defence.

> Adwoa reported that the marriage resulted in the birth of four children. During the marriage her husband cultivated a cocoa farm and made a gift of it to her in circumstances which resulted in misunderstanding and finally divorce. At the time of the gift the children were all below 9 years of age. (Adwoa Krah v. Kwaku Yeboah, Circuit Court, Sunyani, 1970)

The problem of child maintenance was mentioned by one husband in his defence statement.

> The former wife claimed that the marriage lasted thirty-two years during which five children were born and she and her husband jointly cultivated four cocoa farms. The husband, on the other hand, claimed that the farms were made with the help of all his wives, of which he had seven at the time of his marriage to the plaintiff, and three more since the dissolution of that marriage. Since he was maintaining all his twenty-two children, he claimed he could not take on any further responsibilities. (Afua Manu v. Kwadwo Akwa, Sunyani High Court, 1970)

The problem of compensation is obviously considerably complicated by polygyny and successive marriage. As observed at Dominase, farmers who were older and more established were likely to have more than one wife, and for many husbands and wives it was not their first marriage.

In general, wives were likely to consider that they themselves had rights in farms independent of anything their offspring might have received, or of any claims of maintenance for offspring or themselves. This was so even where, as above, the parties were no longer married, or as in the following case where the former husband had died. Nevertheless, wives may be regarded by others as only having rights on behalf of their offspring.

> Akua stated that she helped her husband to make three cocoa farms, one of which was the subject of the dispute. Shortly before he died, it was agreed between her and her late spouse that the farm should be divided and half given to her. Following this, a meeting was called and in the presence of several witnesses including the defendant and the head of the plaintiff's family, the late husband openly declared the gift. In his defence, the heir claimed that he had not dispossessed the plaintiff but rather had given portions of the farms to the plaintiff's five sons. (Akua Saah v. Kwaku Sampane, Kumasi High Court, 1964)

Wives were more likely than offspring to refer to reasons for the gift of farms rather than to emphasise the procedure involved in gift giving. Assistance given in the development of property was often mentioned, as in the cases to which reference has already been made. Hence wives did not refer to farms gifted by will but rather, like the women at Dominase, they claimed that they received these farms during their husbands' working lives. This contrast between mothers and their offspring would seem to reflect the difference in the amount of help that each party was able to give to their respective husbands and fathers, and again supports the information from Dominase. The frequency of divorce was not a question that featured strongly in the Dominase cases but it could be that, anticipating divorce, husbands were reluctant to make provision for wives. Nevertheless, even though divorce is common, the amount of assistance given prior to divorce can be quite considerable, as reported in the case of Abenaa Appeah v. Yaw Kumi recorded at the Sunyani High Court in 1969. Here the marriage had lasted thirty years during which time Abenaa had helped her husband to acquire twenty-three 'seasonal cocoa farms'. Following this he gave his wife a plot of land to develop; however, he was reclaiming this land following divorce.

Four divorcees claimed that the land they were farming had not been given to them by their husbands. Three referred to the source of the land and in each case the parties were cross-cousins. Here the land was provided by the woman's mother's brother and father to her husband and, as would be expected therefore in such a situation, each party was claiming, doubtless correctly, that the land was given to them (Yaw Bogo v. Yaw Serwaah, Circuit Court, Sunyani, 1968, Kwasi Boonyinah v. Yaa Serwaah, Circuit Court, Sunyani, 1968, Ama Kwartimaah v. Kofi Frimpong, District Court, Goaso, 1972).

Women rarely supported their claims by referring to custom, even when discussing gifts, but two divorcees were establishing their rights under Dormaa Customary law, one on the grounds that she, by virtue of assistance given, had acquired such rights. The second was claiming on the grounds that she had been divorced without due cause, although she also mentioned the number of children born and the number of farms she had developed jointly with her spouse (Afua Manu v. Kwadwo Akwa, Sunyani High Court, 1970).

In the suit of Christian Forster Oteng v. Kwadjo Asimeng and Helena Akua Dakwa, High Court, Koforidua, 1973 where reference was again made to arbitration by the Presbyterian Church, the different parties were making claims at the same time, one the widow, the other a member of her spouse's descent group. The widow, in the position of the defence, simply reported that she was entitled to a share of her deceased husband's estate according to Presbyterian Canon Law. The co-defendant, on the other hand, was disputing succession. The heir, however, confirmed his election and argued that since the wife of the deceased was married according to native law and custom, and secondly was not a family member, she had no rights.

In two instances, one involving a woman and the matrikin of her spouse and the other her ex-spouse, the gift made was not in dispute. In one it was the farm boundary that was disputed and in the other the respondent simply denied that he had trespassed on his ex-spouse's land (Akosua Akwaa v. Kwame Adiyia and others, Circuit Court, Kumasi, 1971, and Akua Amoanimah v. Kojo Antwi, District Court, Goaso, 1972).

In contrast again to disputes involving offspring, wives were more frequently in the position of the prosecution rather than the defence since they were often making claims of inadequate provision. In almost a quarter of the disputes involving wives, respondents did not appear, in which case counterclaims were not recorded and possibly settlements were made.

Since wives were claiming rights to farms on the basis of assistance given, counterclaims emphasised their development without help or with assistance from others, and the procedure of gift giving or the gift itself was less likely to be disputed (Table 5.7). However, even gifts of land were challenged, as in the case of Abenaa Appeah to which reference has already been made (Abenaa Appeah v. Yaw Kumi, Sunyani High Court, 1969).

In only one other instance was there any implication that a gift of anything was valid only during or because of the marriage, as in the above case.

> Afua, a divorcee, claimed that she had assisted her husband to farm for sixteen years, following which he built her a house and gave her a farm for which she paid aseda. Both properties were in dispute. Her former husband, on the other hand, stated that he paid for the customary drink on the promise of the wife that her family would return the money. He also argued that the house was only built to 'bring his wife with him' since she was always quarrelling with his family. (Akua Kwatemaa v. Panin Owu-Akyir, District Court, Goaso, 1973.)

TABLE 5.7 Claims against wives and divorcees[a]

Claims	Divorcee v. spouse	Wife v. matrikin of spouse[b]	Divorcee v. matrikin of spouse[b]	Total
Self-acquired farm	4	1	1	6
Denial of gift	2	-	1	3
Wrong procedure for gift	1	1	1	3
Denial of trespass/ disputed boundary	1	1	-	2
Other[c]	1	3	-	4
N = 18				

[a]In five cases claims against wives were not recorded.

[b]Spouse deceased.

[c]Claims that rights of others supersede or are as important as those of spouse including rights of offspring, matrikin and other wives.

Note: Parties may be appearing as prosecution or defence.

Apart from these disputes involving offspring and wives, there were only five other inter-family conflicts, three of which involved offspring of a polygamous union. Among the latter was the only case of offspring being supported in their claim by matrikin of their deceased father. The dispute was not, however, with other matrikin but rather with the half siblings of the defendants. Here again are complications arising out of children of different mothers demanding shares of their father's properties.

> Agnes Ankonam and others, the plaintiffs, claimed that they and their parents made six cocoa farms and built houses. In compensation one farm and one house was given to them following which they paid aseda before witnesses. The defence, P.S. Anhwere and another, one the head of their father's family, stated that in his will, their father gave the house and farm to all his children. (Madam Agnes Ankonam and others v. P.S. Anhwere and another at the Kumasi High Court, 1969)

Similarly, in the case of Kofi Owusu Asanah and others v. D.F. Asare Koranteng and another, heard at the High Court, Accra, in 1965, siblings were demanding equal shares in their father's property on the basis of Akan custom whereas their half siblings were claiming their rights under the provisions of the Marriage Ordinance.

The last of the three cases involving offspring of a polygamous union arose out of an alleged trespass by the heir of two brothers (case first heard 10 March 1972 at the Sunyani High Court).

Lastly, there were two disputes involving in one the offspring of two brothers (T.O. Schandorf v. H.J.F. de Schandorf, Accra High Court, 1967), and in the other an alleged trespass by a man's father's brother (Nana Kwame Nti v. Yaw Biah, District Court, Goaso, 1973). The first is of interest in that this was the only case where a party related the specific amount of money spent on a farm directly to the claim of ownership. Here two men had jointly purchased an already established cocoa farm but since one had contributed twice as much money as the other he was claiming twice the acreage even though, as he pointed out, the certificate of purchase was issued in the joint names of the two purchasers.

INTRA-FAMILY DISPUTES

Litigation between members of the same descent group occurred almost as frequently as that between members of different descent groups. These disputes were for the most part distinctly different from those already discussed, and were often more difficult to categorise since they frequently covered a number of issues at the same time and a variety of litigants including uterine siblings, sisters' sons and mothers' brothers (Table 5.8). The two largest categories of cases included firstly disputes over succession involving competing heirs and secondly disputes over the corporate claims of the descent group involving individual members protecting corporate rights. Only rarely were these individuals making definite claims on the monies involved (Tables 5.9 and 5.10).

TABLE 5.8 Number of disputes within families

Issues	
Disputed gift	9
Disputes over succession	19
Corporate rights in farms[a]	16
Status of property	4
Disputed boundary/ ownership/sale	10
N = 58	

[a]Including individual claims on family property and claims of mismanagement by heirs.

Disputes concerned with the election of heirs to property highlight most vividly the problem of the long-term care of farms and the need for someone to be responsible for the upkeep of what is essentially a corporate concern. In almost one-third of these disputes no supporting reasons were given and in only two were rights supported by reference to inputs in disputed farms. Hence in the case of Osei Akoto v. Kwabena Denteh and another (Circuit Court, Kumasi, 1973), the plaintiff, uterine brother to one of the defendants, was claiming part of a farm established jointly with his

TABLE 5.9 Claims in disputes over succession

Basis of claim/ counterclaim	Number of disputes
Appointment only	7
Inputs in farms	1
Obligations fulfilled	2
Caretaker/ not administrator	5
Appointment terminated/ mismanagement	4
Total	19

TABLE 5.10 Disputes covering rights of heirs

Corporate claims	Individual claims						
	No reply	Valid sale[a]	Personal property	Heir	Seniority	Denial	Pleads guilty
Sale/pledge of family property	5	1	1	-	-	-	1
Family property to be shared	1	-	-	2	1	-	-
Heir not fulfilling obligations	-	-	-	1	-	3	-
N = 16							

[a]Family head and successor agreed.

mother and brothers. The defendants, on the other hand, alleged that they succeeded to the whole farm by right of 'survivorship' and that the plaintiff was not the rightful heir.

Similarly, reference was made in two cases to heirs' fulfilment of their obligations. Thus in J.A. Ashie Kwofie v. Kyere Nyame and another (District Court, Goaso, 1973) the defendant, uterine brother to the deceased, pointed out that he was the only brother who had assisted the deceased on the farm and in addition had paid his brother's debts and aseda following his appointment as heir. In the second case, the right to succeed was disputed on the grounds that the contestant had refused to pay the first owner's debts (Lord Mohammed Akowua v. Alhasan Yaw Marfo, District Court, Goaso, 1973).

Four disputes arose out of an alleged misunderstanding of the task of caretaker on behalf of the descent group and are similar therefore to those already discussed with reference to offspring. The position of caretaker per se, once parties are related in any way, would seem to be precarious from the point of view of all parties involved.

> In the suit of Daniel Kwadjo Danso v. Edward Kwadjo Appiah (Accra High Court, 1974) the plaintiff, first cousin to the deceased, stated he was appointed administrator of the estate of the deceased. In this capacity, and with the approval of the family head, he appointed the defendant to take care of the estate and account to him but did not appoint the defendant as administrator. In his defence, the younger uterine brother of the deceased simply stated that he was appointed customary successor.

The impermanence of the appointment as heir is demonstrated in four disputes where the heir was reported to have been removed for mismanagement, a situation that could eventually lead to the total neglect of a farm, as suggested by the following case.

> The prosecution, the family head, argued that the second defendant was elected to succeed to a property, but following an accusation of mismanagement he abdicated. A second person was elected who also mismanaged, following which a caretaker was hired. In his defence, the first heir claimed that the plaintiff was not a member of the family and therefore had no right to take the case to court. (Akwasi Sasu v. Koranteng and Kwaku Amoah, Circuit Court, Koforidua, 1963).

Following disputes over the position of heir is an almost equally represented group of cases basically concerned with the rights of heirs. These cases further emphasise the limitations on the actions of persons considered to be administrators on behalf of the corporate group rather than owners of farms in their own right. First are four claims that farm proceeds should be shared by all members of the corporate group. In one, a brother was accusing his uterine sister of trespass on a farm that he inherited. His sister in reply confirmed her brother's position as heir, while at the same time pointing out that the property was to be enjoyed by all members of the family (Opanin Kwasi Sikayena v. Madam Adwoa Addai and Barikese Co-op. Society, Circuit Court, Kumasi, 1972).

However, the most important factor leading to conflict in this category was the sale of corporate properties to pay personal debts. These accounted for half the disputes and, as in the example below, none of the prosecution was making a personal claim on the monies involved.

> The plaintiff was the family head, the defendant the heir to a family member. The latter borrowed money, offering the cocoa farms in dispute as security, and since he failed to pay the debt these were auctioned. The plaintiff stated that since the defendant was only a trustee on behalf of the family he had no right to pledge or alienate any of the farms in dispute without the concurrence of the head and other members of the family. (Kwabena Sarkodie Ababio v. Philip Asante and others, Kumasi High Court, 1971)

Sales of land following indebtedness were mentioned in a comparatively large proportion of all the disputes between family members, one in five. The replies to such accusations vary and include claims that the property concerned is of no interest to the group but is rather the personal property of the individual member. Again, as in disputes between heirs, frequently no statement of defence is recorded in the files and in one the respondent pleaded guilty.

> The customary successor to a farm sold it, without reference to the family head, to the second defendant. He later realised he had acted against custom since a successor should not sell the inherited property without the knowledge of the head of the family. (Akosua Mansah and others v. D.K. Yeboah, Circuit Court, Sunyani, 1970)

Not all family members are regarded as having a right to bring such cases involving family properties to court and one defence statement was based on this fact.

> The plaintiff, a junior member of a family, averred that during the illness of the heir to some family property, the family head was plucking the cocoa beans without accounting to anyone, and that he, the plaintiff, had since succeeded to these same properties. In reply, the family head stated that he held the farms in trust for the family and therefore the plaintiff had no right to bring the action, since neither was he head nor had he been authorised by the family to bring the action. (Kwabena Dapaah v. Kwaku Kuma, District Court, Koforidua, 1973)

It has been seen that gifts from fathers to their offspring and wives often result in conflict. Gifts between matrikin are rarely mentioned but may lead to disputes that finally appear before the civil courts for solution. In just over half of the nine cases concerning arguments over farms received as gifts, heirs were making claims that gifted lands were among inherited property while other matrikin were claiming beneficial rights in what they alleged were family farms.

From the records, in making claims to gifts, litigants rarely mentioned any special relationship that may have existed between themselves and the donee, and in only one was there any mention of services rendered. Here it was recorded that the plaintiff was to succeed his younger brother but, since he was family head at the time, a substitute was chosen. Friction arose over money and funeral debts following which the plaintiff destooled himself as head and asked to inherit his brother. The family agreed but the first heir, the defendant, refused to hand over all the properties. In his defence the latter averred that the gun and farm in dispute were given to him for services rendered; he had given his mother's brother money to develop the farm and to buy the gun (Kojo Ntodi on behalf of the family v. Yaw Krah, District Court, Goaso, 1973).

Related to these are four suits involving individual family members claiming farms as personal property on the basis that they established them, and here respondents gave detailed accounts of farm development.

> In the case of Alice Darkoaa and others v. Okwae Feming and another, first heard at the High Court Koforidua in 1972, the first defendant claimed that the property in dispute was acquired by himself as virgin forest. After the death of the first defendant's mother, the co-defendant, her heir, aware of the fact that the disputed farm was not in the mother's estate, never attempted to claim it. The plaintiffs, on the other hand, claimed that the mother gave the land to her only son, the first defendant, to develop in the interest of himself and her other descendants, thereby making it family property.

Finally, a number of conflicts were simply arguments over boundaries or ownership and could be distinguished, at least as far as the records indicate, from any claims concerning the status of the property concerned. Among these was a dispute involving two uterine brothers, one of whom alleged that he did considerable work in farm establishment in the absence of his brother which was not acknowledged. In reply, his brother claimed to have established the farm himself (Opanin Atta Kwabena v. Kramo Seidu, Circuit Court, Sunyani, 1972).

Reading through all the records the investigator is often left with the feeling that disputes will inevitably arise over the ownership and boundaries of cocoa farms that may have been gradually extended or reduced over the years, as was found to be the case with ten Akokoaso holdings investigated by Okali and Kotey (1971). Once a farm has passed through the hands of more than one person it is difficult to trace development - as the following dispute illustrates.

> The plaintiff stated that the farm in dispute was originally acquired as virgin forest by one Akyeampong and developed with Keteku and Sakyibea. When Akyeampong and Sakyibea died the farm was taken over by Keteku as successor. Keteku died and the plaintiff succeeded, the farm coming to him for the benefit of himself and other members of his family. However he was an invalid and therefore gave the farm to the defendant to caretake

and render account, which he had refused to do for the past eight years; he was now claiming the property as his own. The defendant claimed that the farm was actually purchased by his late mother who asked Akyeampong to assist her. Since she failed to pay the full purchase price of the land the defendant paid the balance and thus ownership vested in him. (Atta Kofi v. Richard Ebenezer Kwaku Akyea, District Court, Koforidua, 1973.)

Many of the details concerning the sources of farms given in the court records resemble those given by the farmers at Akokoaso covered in Chapter 4. Farmers gave reports of farm development that were often full of apparently contradictory statements and vague references to farms. The Dominase respondents were much clearer, largely because the farms to which reference was being made were younger.

DISCUSSION

Although exact details of the ages of farms are not given in the files, the records do suggest that disputes cover cocoa farms of all ages and include farms located in both new and old cocoa areas. Overall the data support and enlarge upon a number of the issues already highlighted and suggest other factors of importance.

The principal feature of the court cases was that conflicts over cocoa farms did not arise from attempts to change the customary rules nor from the ambiguity or uncertainty of customary rules, but rather from the multiple interests in farms. Thus the only distinct references to the distribution of returns contrary to customary arrangements occurred in the three cases where litigants based their claims on rulings of the Presbyterian Church or the Marriage Ordinance. This conclusion is not contradicted by the frequency with which litigation occurs within descent groups. Tensions and conflicts between matrikin are now well documented, and disputes over farms may be causes or expressions of already existing tensions. The fact that such disputes appear in the civil courts is also not in itself significant since prior to the opening of the civil courts, disputes are likely to have been settled by other means. In this connection it is interesting to note that in only one-third of the cases recorded had any judgment actually been given; disputes were more likely to be withdrawn or to be settled out of court (Table 5.11).

With respect to the multiple interests in farms, the court cases substantiate the information from the Dominase farmers among whom it was demonstrated that, although the elementary family unit was significant as a source of labour for men in mobile settings, they continued also to rely on matrikin. A number used the proceeds of inherited property for making settlement in the pioneer area possible, and one farmer was able to utilise his ties with affines, who were citizens. Female farmers, on the other hand, were more isolated in terms of the variety of assistance received. Thus, overall, strangers and citizens were shown to be similar with respect to their reliance on others for cocoa farm development.

TABLE 5.11 Cases finalised in court

	Case finalised %	Pending/ discontinued %	Total %	Number of cases
Inter-family dispute	38.7	61.3	100.0	62
Intra-family dispute	32.8	67.2	100.0	58
Other	-	100.0	100.0	2
N = 122				

This variety in sources of inputs for land development and sources of cocoa farms themselves is also confirmed by the following information from a different sample of farmers in Ashanti (see Appendix 4). Here 9 per cent of the farmers claimed that they had received money for farm development, one woman from her husband and children, another from her children alone. The men received assistance from a wider variety of persons, in two instances from their fathers, two from matrikin and the last from affines. Almost half the men had inherited cocoa farms (Table 5.12) and, as was observed in the cases of Kwesi Poku and Kofi Owusu at Dominase, such farms can be important sources of finance for future investment even though returns from these farms may also be used for maintaining wives and offspring of the deceased and matrikin. Cash is of particular importance in mobile areas and the majority of the Ashanti farmers used money from the proceeds of their own mature farms to finance farm developments away from home. Thus only two farmers of the twenty, all male, who reported that they had paid anything to secure farming rights, received financial assistance from relatives, one from his father and the second from matrikin. Overall therefore, these farmers were similar to their counterparts at Dominase who used proceeds from bearing farms in their home towns to establish themselves in the pioneer area. The Ashanti farmers were more likely to report that they had received help from relatives in the form of labour and two-thirds had either received such assistance in the past or were still receiving it (Table 5.13). For the men, matrikin, followed by wives possibly accompanied by offspring, had given most help in terms of the number of farms on which they had worked. Women were as likely to have received assistance from spouses as offspring.

Under these circumstances, the proposition that cocoa farming is associated with the isolation of the conjugal unit was not sustained. At the same time it was shown that all those who invested in the farms at Dominase either expected to be compensated, directly or indirectly, or were themselves fulfilling an obligation to assist, possibly out of past help that they had received. Thus the distribution of returns, including the inheritance of the property itself, did not always reflect investments in farms.

TABLE 5.12 How cocoa farms were acquired by owners

	Males			Females		
	Age in years			Age in years		
	26-44	45-64	65+	25-44	45-64	65+
	%	%	%	%	%	%
Self-acquired and/or gift only	40.0	37.5	47.6	-	75.0	66.7
Self-acquired or gift and inherited	-	54.2	47.6	-	8.3	-
Inherited farms only	60.0	8.3	4.8	100.0	16.7	33.3
Total	100.0	100.0	100.0	100.0	100.0	100.0
Number of farm owners	5	24	21	1	12	3

TABLE 5.13 Labour received from relatives on cocoa farms, past and present

	Male owners	Female owners	All farm owners
	%	%	%
Spouse ± offspring	24.5	45.4	28.1
Offspring/ grandchildren	13.2	45.4	18.8
Matrikin	52.8	-	43.8
Other[a]	5.7	9.2	6.2
No reply	3.8	-	3.1
Total	100.0	100.0	100.0
Number of farms	53	11	64
Number of farmers reported receiving assistance	41	8	49

Two farmers reported that many people had helped them, and two that their in-laws had.

The Ashanti farmers were also asked about various exchanges in which they had been involved, including exchanges in business activities other than farming and schooling (Table 5.14). Although all respondents claimed that they were paying for their own children's school fees, 38 per cent were also paying for matrikin. Few were

TABLE 5.14 Assistance received and given by cocoa farmers

	Assistance given				Assistance received		
	On farms		Schooling[a]		Schooling		Business
	Males %	Females %	Males %	Females %	Males %	Females %	Males %
None	46.0	31.1	52.0	81.2			80.0
Spouse		25.0					
Sibling	2.0		4.0		22.2		
Mother's brother	22.0				22.2		20.0
Mother		25.0					
Father	16.0	6.3			44.5	100.0	
Parents and mother's brother	8.0	6.3			11.1		
Sister's children			40.0	12.5			
Other relatives	6.0	6.3	4.0	6.3			
Other persons not related	100.0	100.0	100.0	100.0	100.0	100.0	100.0
Total number of persons	50	16	50	16	9	3	5
N = 66							

[a]Excluding own offspring. All farmers with children of school age reported that they were paying the fees.

themselves educated but again, among those who were, matrikin were also important for men whereas the school fees of the women had all been paid for by their fathers. In contrast to the help given with school fees, only six farmers, five males and one female, reported having assisted matrikin in business, all of whom were siblings. In both these areas women were less likely to have assisted than their male counterparts. Overall, as demonstrated by the information from Akokoaso and Dominase, female farmers were less wealthy at all ages than their male counterparts, both in terms of the number of cocoa farms owned and production, and they were therefore less likely to be in a position to assist others (Tables 5.15 and 5.16).

Farmers were more likely to have been involved in exchanges of labour on farms than of assistance in business or schooling, and in this area women were more involved than men. Hence just over 50 per cent of the male and almost 70 per cent of the female farmers had worked for relatives at one time or another, mostly before they had started their own farms. Matrikin featured significantly among the men as with assistance that they themselves had received. None reported having worked on their wives' farms whereas the women had assisted both their spouses and their mothers equally.

The fact that inputs in farms are not always linked with returns, and that individuals are not always therefore claiming rights in farms by virtue of investments made is confirmed by the court cases. They also provide valuable insight into the items involved in the exchanges. Thus farms were most commonly given to persons who had no direct inheritance rights; recipients included sisters' daughters who appeared to have contributed little or nothing to farm work, and sisters' sons, offspring and wives, some of whom had worked closely on farms with the owners. Among the Dominase farmers, wives were the only persons who were in a position to have assisted with labour on farms over a comparatively long period of time. In accordance with this finding, wives were also more likely than other relatives to refer to assistance that they had given on farms to support their claims in court. However, the number of children issuing from a marriage, services performed, and even debts paid, were also mentioned - demonstrating that farms can not be looked at in isolation.

Throughout the analysis of the organisation of cocoa production among the Dominase farmers, it was emphasised that all those assisting on farms who were expecting direct reciprocation could be disappointed. The court cases demonstrate that even if they are compensated by gifts of land or farms, these can be disputed. Gifts per se are a subject of controversy regardless of who the recipients are and the basis of their claims. At Dominase, only one woman had actually finalised any gift exchange: Kofi Owusu's wife, following her husband's death. Since the procedure of gift giving was frequently referred to by litigants in courts, this is a serious omission. It is therefore relevant to ask how significant gifts of farms are among the Ashanti farmers.

Among these, two-thirds of all the farms owned were self-acquired or self-developed; the remainder were more likely to have been inherited than received as gifts (Table 5.17). In total only twelve farmers reported that they had received farms as gifts, seven women and five men. (Among the women, brothers or mother's brothers

TABLE 5.15 Distribution of cocoa farms per owner

Cocoa farms per owner	Male owners 25-44 %	45-64 %	65+ %	All ages %	Female owners 25-44 %	45-64 %	65+ %	All ages %
One	60.0	8.3	4.9	12.0	-	25.0	33.3	25.0
Two	20.0	25.0	19.0	22.0	100.0	66.7	33.3	62.5
Three	20.0	37.5	19.0	28.0	-	8.3	-	6.3
Four	-	12.5	19.0	14.0	-	-	33.4	6.2
Five	-	12.5	9.5	10.0	-	-	-	-
Six and over	-	4.2	28.6	14.0	-	-	-	-
Total	100.0	100.0	100.0	100.0	100.0	100.0	100.0	100.0
Number of farms	5	24	21	50	1	12	3	16

TABLE 5.16 Distribution of farmers by cocoa production

	Male owners			All	Female owners			All
	25-44	45-64	65+	ages	25-44	45-64	65+	ages
	%	%	%	%	%	%	%	%
Less than average production	80.0	37.5	38.1	42.0	100.0	75.0	100.0	81.3
More than average production	-	45.8	57.1	46.0	-	8.3	-	6.2
No production information	20.0	16.7	4.8	12.0	-	16.7	-	12.5
Total	100.0	100.0	100.0	100.0	100.0	100.0	100.0	100.0
Number of farmers	5	24	21	50	1	12	3	16

TABLE 5.17 Means by which cocoa farms acquired

	Male owners %	Female owners %	All farm owners %
Self-acquired	67.2	58.1	65.9
Inherited	24.9	9.7	22.7
Gift from parents	5.8	12.9	6.8
Gift from spouse	-	6.4	1.0
Gift from mother's brother	-	12.9	1.8
Other[a]	2.1	-	1.8
Total	100.0	100.0	100.0
Number of farms	189	31	220

[a]Farms acquired by strangers from the Chief.

featured most as sources of such farms followed by spouses and, in one instance, a father. Men were most likely to have received theirs from their fathers, followed by their mothers.) However, survey data based on a different and larger sample in three areas of Ashanti suggest that gift giving is more significant than indicated here, particularly as a source of farms for women, and strongly support the view that such transfers can be made successfully (Table 5.18).

TABLE 5.18 How cocoa farms were acquired by owners

Method of acquisition	Mampong Male %	Mampong Female %	Konongo Male %	Konongo Female %	Bekwai Male %	Bekwai Female %
Planted self	39.3	33.5	56.4	40.0	54.7	36.8
Purchased self	13.4	4.7	1.5	3.2	7.3	6.9
Inherited	17.1	10.3	15.9	5.9	20.6	14.2
Gift	26.1	48.5	19.7	42.2	13.1	39.7
Other	-	-	6.5	8.7	-	-
No reply	4.1	3.0	-	-	4.3	2.4
Total	100.0	100.0	100.0	100.0	100.0	100.0
Number of farms	643	233	593	184	714	246

Source: Okali, Gyekye and Mabey (1974), p. 93.

The court records do, however, point to additional problems with gifts. Firstly, recipients do not always have immediate rights to all the farm proceeds; farms given to offspring, for instance, might be used to defray their father's funeral expenses. Secondly, individuals are frequently accused of making gifts of corporate property. The court cases therefore highlight the fact that corporate rights in farms may also be insecure.

The position of wives and offspring as recipients of gifts is made particularly insecure by the impermanence and multiplicity of marriage contracts, although none of the women claiming gifts in court were new wives. Relevant to the question of the security of the claims of wives is the comment of the presiding magistrate in the case of Adwoa Krah v. Kwaku Yeboah, first heard at the Circuit Court, Sunyani, in 1970, that once a gift had been given by a man to his wife he was presumed to have no further interest in it.

The whole question of the gifts of farms to wives raises the issue of the economic independence of women, a discussion started earlier when documenting arrangements for gift giving among the Dominase farmers. As noted, the finalisation of a gift exchange may be regarded as the end of assistance given by a wife, or if it is related to offspring born, the end of child bearing. Overall, however, the economic rights of wives are not clear. The lack of joint property holding between spouses is mentioned in the literature of the Akan, for instance, but little reference is made to the duties of wives other than as child bearers, and even then it is the close bond between mothers and offspring that is stressed. Some reference was made to the rights and domestic responsibilities of wives in the court records. The position of married women was described most succinctly in the summing up by one magistrate as follows: 'Plaintiff did not farm together with her late husband in the sense of joint farmers but that being a wife, she lived with her husband while he was farming' (Madam Afua Achiaa v. Madam Yaa Aboraa, District Court, Goaso, 1972). Ollennu (1959) states that it is the domestic responsibility of a wife and children to assist a man and writes elsewhere that 'By customary law, the children of a wife being dependants of a man, family life requires that a son should work with and for his father, and a wife with and for her husband, and property acquired with such assistance is the individual property of the man' (Ollennu, 1962: 39-40). This type of argument is, however, inadquate for explaining the behaviour of wives. Married women at both Akokoaso and Dominase did operate independently of their spouses even though these data and those presented for Ashanti farmers demonstrate that they had a lower rate of participation in cocoa farming than men. This is not contradicted at Dominase by the apparently greater dependence of wives on husbands. Thus although the question of gifts of land or farms and other returns apart from food crops did not arise when their husbands were building up their cocoa holding, and wives at this point did appear to be in a particularly dependent position, this was also the time when they were bearing children, and when, therefore, in any setting they would have concentrated on the growing of food crops. By remaining with their spouses during this period, and planting the spouses' farms rather than their own, as would be the case in their home areas, they were also investing in their own future security, since husbands are a source of farms for women. Certainly all the data presented both from Akokoaso and Dominase suggests that wives expected some return, although rarely did they claim that they had established a joint economic concern. Thus at Dominase, the women were perfectly aware of the assistance, at least in the form of labour on farms, given by matrikin, and the mature farms were regarded as being for the men. Their expectations of some return would also appear to have a foundation in customary law. Thus Bentsi-Enchill (1964) writes that 'It is a rule that expenditure of labour creates rights' (p. 109). Ollennu would however argue that they thereby receive rights to maintenance (Ollennu, 1959).

It is therefore relevant to ask at what point a wife, as distinct from an unmarried woman, is able to work on her own. This question can again be followed from the Ashanti farmers. In total, forty-eight farmers, almost half of whom had more than one wife at the time of the survey, gave information on their wives. Wives were divided into discrete categories according to whether they were working separately or jointly with their spouses on their farms, or independently in a non-farm occupation. Approximately 60 per cent of the wives were working independently of their spouses and there was no indication that this work pattern was associated with the age of wives (Table 5.19), whereas it did appear to be linked with polygyny, although not with the position of wives in terms of seniority (Table 5.20). The incidence of separate work arrangements also increased with the age of the husband (Table 5.21), which is consistent with the finding that cocoa farm ownership increases with age. This is also the time when farmers are likely to have more than one wife. Thus Adjoa Owusuwa at Dominase, who spent all her time on her own farms, was the sixth wife of her husband, who was sixty years old and had many established cocoa farms. On the whole, women with co-wives at Dominase travelled more frequently and had more opportunity to engage in their own separate activities.

TABLE 5.19 Occupation of farmers' wives by age of wives

	Age of wife in years				
	15-24	25-44	45-64	65+	No reply
	%	%	%	%	%
Works independent of spouse	50.0	28.6	31.8	50.0	55.2
Works jointly with spouse	50.0	71.4	68.2	50.0	44.8
Total	100.0	100.0	100.0	100.0	100.0
Number of women	4	21	22	2	29
N = 78					

TABLE 5.20 Polygyny and economic status of wives

	One wife %	Two or more wives Senior %	2nd %	3rd %	4th %
Works independent of spouse	20.0	52.2	47.8	60.0	50.0
Works jointly with spouse	80.0	47.8	52.2	40.0	50.0
Total	100.0	100.0	100.0	100.0	100.0
Number of women N = 78	25	23	23	5	2

TABLE 5.21 Occupation of farmers' wives by age of farmer

	Age of farmer in years 25-44 %	45-64 %	65+ %
Wives work only separately	20.0	25.0	36.8
Wives work only jointly	80.0	66.7	47.4
Wives working jointly and separately	-	8.3	15.8
Total	100.0	100.0	100.0
Number of farmers	5	24	19

Husbands were also asked to specify the actual farms on which their wives worked, and just over one in every four who were reported to be joint workers were working on food farms only. However, these replies were inconsistent with details given about labour arrangements on particular farms (Table 5.22). Here wives were reported to be working only on their husbands' food farms. They may, of course, have assisted on the cocoa farms in the past, as suggested earlier.

In interpreting other data from Ashanti, Okali and Mabey (1975) refer to Fortes (1970), who observed that although in theory women have the same economic opportunities as men, in general the responsibilities of motherhood are a handicap to economic achievement while the children are young. They also demonstrate that once women

TABLE 5.22 Labour arrangements on farms

	Male owners		Female owners	
	Cocoa farms %	Food farms %	Cocoa farms %	Food farms %
Self	7.4	28.6	29.1	89.5
Offspring only	2.6	7.1	12.9	10.5
Matrikin only	9.0	2.4	3.2	-
In-laws	1.1	-	3.2	-
Hired labour/ government	78.3	-	51.6	-
Self/spouse/ offspring	-	33.3	-	-
No reply	1.6	28.6	-	-
Total	100.0	100.0	100.0	100.0
Number of farms	189	42	31	19

start cocoa farming they are unlikely to be in a position where they are still required to assist others. As shown by the data here, this is more likely to occur in polygynous situations that are linked with the economic success of husbands, and (from information given in Chapter 3 from Akokoaso and Dominase) when they are no longer married, suggesting that economic independence, although related to fertility status, depends ultimately on the marital situation.

Returning to the question of the security of expectations of direct returns to investment made in farms, among the various production arrangements at Dominase, that comprising a man and his sister's son was identified as being particularly insecure. On the other hand, two sets of persons had been given farms to caretake, and it was noted that this was a particularly suitable means of assisting others in their move toward economic independence, without placing them in a subordinate position or involving them in any further need to reciprocate. The court cases demonstrate, however, that this system may be open to abuse. How far this problem supports the use of hired labourers as caretakers of bearing farms is difficult to say, but certainly few bearing farms are left entirely to the responsibility of relatives. Thus the Ashanti farmers used hired labour on two-thirds of their cocoa farms not being operated by the government, regardless of the age of the farm (Table 5.23). Although few farms owned by the Ashanti farmers were being cared for by offspring or matrikin alone, one case involving a farm cared for by a man's sister's son was reported to be in court. Inherited farms were more likely to be cared for by matrikin or hired caretakers than those acquired by the farmers themselves or received as gifts (Table 5.24).

TABLE 5.23 Labour arrangements on cocoa farms by age of trees

	Male owners: Ages of trees in years				Female owners: Ages of trees in years			
	1-10	11-20	21+	No reply	1-10	11-20	21+	No reply
	%	%	%	%	%	%	%	%
Self	14.6	8.9	4.1	-	22.2	50.0	14.3	100.0
Offspring only	4.9	-	3.1	-	11.1	-	28.6	-
Matrikin only	4.9	13.3	6.2	50.0	-	-	14.3	-
In-laws	2.4	-	1.0	-	-	-	14.2	-
Hired labour/ government	73.2	75.6	85.6	16.7	66.7	50.0	28.6	-
No reply	-	2.2	-	33.3	-	-	-	-
Total	100.0	100.0	100.0	100.0	100.0	100.0	100.0	100.0
Number of farms	41	45	97	6	18	4	7	2

N = 220

TABLE 5.24 Labour arrangements on cocoa farms by means acquired

	Means acquired					
	Self-acquired %	Inherited %	Gift from parents %	Gift from spouse[a] %	Gift from mother's brother %	Other %
Self	11.7	2.0	33.3	-	-	-
Offspring only	6.2	-	-	-	-	-
Matrikin only	6.2	14.0	-	50.0	-	25.0
In-laws	1.4	-	-	-	-	-
Hired labour/government	72.4	84.0	66.7	50.0	75.0	75.0
No reply	2.1	-	-	-	25.0	-
Total	100.0	100.0	100.0	100.0	100.0	100.0
Number of farms	145	50	15	2	4	4
N = 220						

[a] Wives from husbands.

Thus customary property relations are important for determining the way in which cocoa properties are organised throughout, both when the individual appears to have supreme control and when the descent group definitely has control following inheritance. The attempt to cut off two discrete periods of time is unnecessary and even confusing when trying to understand how production is organised among the Akan.

As noted in the discussion of returns among the Dominase farmers, of particular relevance to the position of matrikin in dependent economic positions assisting on farms is the fact that exchanges between descent group members are not necessarily direct. This is clearly indicated in the court cases by the fact that in making claims to property, representatives of the corporate unit rarely refer to inputs on farms. These data therefore question the way in which decisions are made regarding rights in immovable property, as reported by Brokensha (1966) and Woodman (1966); that is, by reference to the help that has been received by others. Throughout the court cases presented here, there is a presumption by litigants in favour of the corporate concern which is also contrary to the judgments of the superior courts as reported by Woodman (1966), among which presumptions in favour of family property were already weakening in 1935. A similar presumption in favour of corporate rights was observed among the farmers at Dominase, even when individuals appeared to have developed their properties alone. Thus Kwadwo Kusi, who said that those who could have helped him had died before he got around to asking, was concerned to provide all his potential heirs with land before attempting to do the same for his offspring.

We have seen that corporate rights in farms are developed through chain generalised exchange. It is this fact that makes all direct exchange claims between relatives, including wives, offspring and matrikin, which are not immediately reciprocated, insecure.

Chapter 6

Conclusion

The transfer from subsistence to cash crop production without doubt creates dramatic changes in the economic relationships of farmers, as can be seen from this study of Akan cocoa farmers. In many situations, contractual exchanges with unrelated persons supersede those based on affective or other ties. Nevertheless, such relationships are used to satisfy only some of the farmer's requirements and the allocations of inputs, particularly labour, cannot be explained by reference to their relative prices.

Agricultural changes reflect ongoing changes in other sectors of the economy, all of which are directed towards a reallocation of productive resources from customary sources to the open market. Consequently, numerous commentators on the contemporary scene have predicted, and even demonstrated, the breakdown of customary units of economic co-operation, which among the Akan, as in other societies practising matrilineal inheritance and descent, are corporate descent groups. The most significant change identified is the emergence of the elementary family as the most important unit of economic co-operation, as evidenced mainly by the composition of residence and production units and the increase in transfers of property by gift as distinct from inheritance. Among cocoa farmers, the migrant or stranger was viewed as the supreme example of modern man in rural communities, and the migration itself was shown to be a predominantly male affair. In this, reports of cocoa farmers correspond with others which show that persons living in urban and mobile situations in general are particularly subject to change.

It is clear that the increasing importance of marital ties for residence and farming is a function of mobility. However, closeness between spouses in these two respects was not always associated with mobility, as was evident at Akokoaso, a settled community, where a number of citizens were both residing and working together on the same farms. Nevertheless, joint farm ownership did not materialise from this co-operation either among strangers or citizens; rather wives were likely to be in a dependent position working on their husbands' farms. This pattern was particularly pronounced among strangers, and female strangers contrasted vividly, therefore, with their citizen counterparts. A number of women had even profited as citizens by marrying strangers who thereby became the dependent party, and assisted with their wives' farm development.

Both men and women could, however, aspire to farm ownership, and it was therefore the changing role of members of the labour force throughout life that was found to be of vital importance for understanding the real significance of the economic relationship between members of production units, in particular spouses, but also offspring and matrikin. All started their farming life as assistants rather than farm owners, and hence the position of an assistant to a relative, including that of a wife to her husband, was regarded as temporary, although not everyone was able to rise to farm ownership. Overall, however, women were more involved in food production than men and acquired their own first farms, albeit food farms, before their male counterparts. During marriage, wives assisted their spouses, at least for some time and regardless of the setting in which they were living. While men were able to start developing their cocoa holdings from the time of marriage with the help of their wives and others, women had to wait until later when their children were grown. Although therefore wives could aspire to cocoa farm ownership, it was women who were older, and frequently no longer married, who were more likely to reach this position.

The continued importance of customary economic co-operation between matrikin even in areas away from home, and therefore in situations that were most ideal for the individual wishing to operate in isolation from matrikin, was revealed by covering the various farm investments by men, women, husbands, wives, offspring and matrikin over time. Unlike the farmers described by Gough (1952), migrants were not giving up their ancestral lands but rather making use of them for establishing more farms in pioneer areas. Indeed the migrant situation itself was regarded as temporary - as both Field (1960) and Hill (1963) demonstrated for the Akwapim migrants working in Akim Abuakwa.

Clearly Busia's contention based on research completed in the 1940s that the cocoa industry had grown as a result of individual toil and enterprise, or that all the work had been done by the farmer assisted by his wives and children or by hired labour paid for by himself was not confirmed. The conclusions in this work correspond with those of Fortes (1950), Caldwell (1968), Van de Geest (1974), and Oppong (1972), all of whom have demonstrated the continued importance of customary rights and duties based upon matrilineal descent even in urban areas and among the educated in Ghana. They also support the findings of Handwerker (1973) among traders in Monrovia, and Berry (1975) among cocoa farmers in Nigeria, that organised kin groups play an important positive role in promoting business activities, and provide an alternative view to that of Lanfranchi (1962) and Okali and Kotey (1971) of a negative relationship between the operation of matrilineal rules of inheritance and the long-term care of cocoa farms although the court cases suggest the need for further work. Suggestions that this situation arises from neglecting the functions of the maximal lineage while stressing economic factors as the primary cause of the breakdown of the lineage where it has occurred may be important. Thus Goody was noted in Chapter 1 as mentioning the significance of political functions.

Although matrikin were important even for migrant farmers, elementary family units were the most significant sources of labour for men. Nevertheless there was some division of labour that continued to reflect the ideal of separate property development of spouses and fathers and sons. Women in particular were continuing with a work pattern already identified at Akokoaso, one that restricted them to food rather than cocoa production, and this fact alone placed their contribution to their husband's farm development on a temporary basis. It also appeared to confirm Boserup's view of women being confined to the subsistence sector while men concentrated on the cash crops (Boserup, 1970). At Dominase, both elementary family units and the husband's matrikin were engaged in farm development, while it was acknowledged that the property was for the man. This placed the actors in a potentially insecure economic position and one that conflicted both with the norm of separating ties of marriage, parenthood and descent, and the customary position of women in matrilineal societies. Fortes (1971) observes that comparisons of patrilineal and matrilineal family systems on a world-wide basis show that one of the key differences relates to the social and legal position of women as sisters and daughters, wives and mothers. In societies practising matrilineal inheritance and descent, women traditionally have a degree of economic, political and legal equality with men and a status of dignity that was never accorded their sisters in classical patrilineal family systems.

The first claims on farms were made by descent groups since throughout farm development there was a recognition that it was corporate property that was being developed. Obligations acquired throughout life could only be satisfied when the farmers themselves were well established, and hence only the more successful farmers at Dominase had even started to make arrangements for the future of the offspring, wives and dependent matrikin who were working with them. At the same time, other obligations were also being met and these were principally, although not always, those arising from descent group membership itself.

Associated with this changed economic status was a change in marital and other relations. Thus farmers who could acknowledge their obligations to matrikin were able to operate more independently since they were no longer in a subordinate position. In contrast to what was suggested by Long (1968), therefore, the situation where individuals in business no longer felt the need to depend on their matrikin was not regarded as a breakdown point between themselves and the corporate group, but rather a point where the relationship itself changed in form. The position of wives also changed as the husband aged and expanded his holdings. As farms increased both in age and size the relative contribution of the labour of wives decreased. The more successful farmers had more than one wife and these wives were able to operate relatively independently. Nevertheless, they, like their husbands before them, needed assistance with their farm investment and expected to receive this start from their husbands. The view that it is husbands who are attempting to leave farms to wives and offspring in contemporary economic settings so forcibly stressed by writers documenting change, is therefore not confirmed by this study. Rather wives were themselves expecting their services to be reciprocated, and thus, like the Yoruba women in Nigeria, were demanding payments, although not before themselves giving assistance (Galletti, Baldwin and Dina, 1956). If none was given and they felt that they had alternatives, divorce would ensue.

In view of the fact that men could not fulfil their obligations unless they were successful, it is relevant to ask what determines success. The fact that individuals at Dominase were maintaining ties with numerous relatives had considerable economic advantage in the migrant situation. Marwick (1956), writing of the matrilineal Cewa, observes that people who lack relatives are objects of pity and scorn and the position of such people in Akokoaso and Dominase may be economically precarious. Thus it was the younger men, women and strangers who were not in a position to call on a wide variety of relatives to assist them with labour. The most successful farmers at Dominase had each retained close economic ties with matrikin. However, farmers and their assistants used all their resources to advantage, which at times even involved them in situations that contrasted sharply with custom. Thus the women at Dominase were almost completely dependent on their husbands even with respect to the production of food crops, while stranger men married to Akokoaso citizens were dependent upon their wives. Others were using links with affines, for instance, all contrary to custom. Nevertheless, all these relationships were explicable in terms of the alternatives available at the time in particular settings. Strangers are usually faced with a narrow range of relatives with whom they might live. At both Akokoaso and Dominase they were more likely to be living with spouses than their local counterparts, whereas on returning home they might revert to living according to custom. As Barth (1967) himself shows, it is not necessary therefore to hypothesise a changed categorisation of values to explain a changing pattern of activities. It is possible to look at changed circumstances that may well make other allocations optimal when evaluated by the same standards. Hence both husbands and wives at Dominase were aware of the establishment of corporate property but each stood to gain from co-operation at a certain point in time. Fathers and sons were also working closely together, each again standing to gain. Nevertheless, sons could be disappointed and fathers would take them to court if they attempted to claim more than they felt was their right.

Many of the studies of the changing West African scene have been concerned with establishing the path of change itself, and frequently, by focusing on a particular aspect of production at a particular point in time, hypothesise a complete break with the old in the face of economic changes. In this study, all aspects of production and the roles that people have played have been analysed over time, thus revealing an underlying continuity of values. In addition, it has been shown that cocoa farming cannot be viewed in isolation and indeed the very insecurity of the individual claims of wives, offspring and dependent matrikin on men's farms, and gifts of farms to these same people, derived from this fact. Conceptually, this situation where different types of exchanges impinge on one another and where one of these involves a corporate unit, is not catered for by the exchanges outlined in Chapter 2 and emphasises the need for further studies of the circumstances underlying different exchanges.

Thus synchronic analysis of particular farm investments is inadequate for exploring the changing roles that individuals or corporate units are playing in the modern sector. By using different techniques, this work has documented how farmers can further their interests in different situations where the environment constrains to change. As Frankenberg (1967) argues, individuals and societies are not passive recipients to exogenous pushes in the form of technological changes.

Appendix 1

Residence and production units at Akokoaso and Dominase

Interview Schedule

Compound information

1 Age and sex of compound head
2 Number of residents

For each person fifteen years and over not schooling

1 Ethnic group
2 Age
3 Sex
4 Education: number of years, standard reached, place last schooled
5 Home town
6 Home town of mother
7 Home town of father
8 Date of arrival at present residence
9 Date of expected departure from present residence
10 Relationship to compound head and other compound members
11 Present occupation. If farmer, state whether:
(a) Farm owner/assistant to relative (specify)/hired worker
If owner, state:
(b) Crops grown
(c) Source of farms
(d) Labour arrangements on farms
(e) Location of farms
(f) Age when owner started to work independently
12 Assistance given on other people's farms in the past
13 Previous occupations
14 Married persons - residence of spouse

Offspring not working but resident in the compound

15 Sex
16 Age
17 School/under school age

Other persons under fifteen or fifteen+ resident in compound but not working

18 Age
19 Sex
20 Relationship to compound members

All offspring of residents

21 Age
22 Sex
23 Place of residence
24 Relationship to people with whom they are staying
25 Occupation/schooling

Non-resident spouses

26 Ethnic group
27 Home town of mother
28 Home town of father
29 Birthplace
30 Present residence
31 Present occupation
If farmer, state whether:
(a) Farm owner/assistant to relative (specify)/hired worker
If owner, state:
(b) Crops grown
(c) Source of farms

Appendix 2

Farm management survey at Dominase

Farm Survey

Name of farm owner and caretaker if owner is absent................
....

Farm survey data-cocoa farms

1 Distance of the farm from the village...........................
2 Direction of the farm from the village..........................
3 Size of the farm.....................
4 Age of the farm......................
5 Age of the trees.....................
6 Estimate of the number of trees on the farm.....................
7 Number and type of large shade trees............................
....
....
8 Type of cocoa tree...................
9 Type of cover (nurse) crop of young cocoa.......................
....
10 Condition of the farm, pests and diseases......................
....
11 Condition of the farm, maintenance at point of initial survey
....
....
12 Slope of the farm....................
13 Drainage of the farm...
14 Soil type of the farm..
....

Other data:

1 Is there a village on the farm? Yes/No. If Yes, does anyone who works on the farm live there permanently? Yes/No.
2 Is there a nursery for seedlings on the farm? Yes/No.

Notes: Make notes on the surrounding land, i.e. whether forest, abandoned farm, food farm, etc.

Interview Schedule

Name of farm owner:......................Week:....................
Name of respondent:........................
For each day of the week ask:

1 What did you do today? (Farm work/non-farm work/travel/sick/resting/social/other - specify.)
2 If farm work, on whose farm did you work and on what crop; doing what job? (If farm owner's farm, write exactly which farm.)
3 When did you start and when did you finish? (If more than one activity for each day then write each activity.)

Day	Activities	Time Start Finish
Monday		
Tuesday		
Wednesday		
Thursday		
Friday		
Saturday		
Sunday		

Income items from cocoa farm: foodstuffs

Name of farmer:........................ Farm reference:..

Date of inter- view	Item (plantain/ cassava beans/ palm nuts/ wine, etc.)	Quantity harvested	Immediate sale processing[1]	Foodstuffs for sale			Foodstuffs for home consumption		Remarks
				Value when sold ¢	Place of sale	Transport cost	Immediate consumption/ processing	Imputed value	

1 'Processing' includes washing/drying/pounding, etc., NOT preparation for eating.

Income items from cocoa farms: dry cocoa pods

Name of farmer:..............................

Date of interview	Farm reference	Date of sale or transfer of pods to new farm	Item(s) sold/ pods used on own farms	Amount/ no. of pods loads/lb	Where sold/ for pods note where sold or used	Cash receipts	Remarks

Hired labour employment and expenditure

Name of farmer:........................

Date of interview	Farm reference	Number and type of labourer	Date hired	Date left	Work done	Payment made by labourer (if any)	Payment made to labourer (cash and food). Note where food came from, e.g. cocoa farm/food farm/ purchased

Expenditure items on cocoa farms excluding labour (Gammalin/oil/pods/plantain suckers/cutlass/knife/poison/hiring of spraying machine/expenditure on labourers other than actual cash or food payment-medicine/clothing, etc.)

Name of farmer:..................................

Date of interview	Farm reference	Date purchased	Item(s) purchased[1]	Where purchased and from whom	Amount paid ¢	Remarks

1 If transport cost incurred, note amount as a separate item.

Appendix 3

Court records surveyed

	Number of relevant cases	Year in which cases first heard in the court[a]
Accra High Court	7	1965-74
Koforidua High Court	14	1971-4[b]
Kumasi High Court	21	1963-74
Sunyani High Court	21	1966-73
Circuit Court, Koforidua	9	1963-74
Circuit Court, Kumasi	7	1970-3
Circuit Court, Sunyani	21	1963-74
District Court GD.1 Koforidua	3	1969-73
District Court GD.1 Goaso	19	1972-3
Number of cases	122	

[a]The case may also have been heard at another court. Where case still pending and not heard, year refers to date against which the case is recorded in the process book.

[b]The High Court at Koforidua was established in 1970. Before this date all High Court cases falling within the Eastern Region were sent to Accra.

LIST OF CASES

ACCRA HIGH COURT

1965 Kofi Owusu Asanah, Kwame Koranteng, Abena Otiwa and Yaa Korantemaa v. D.F. Asare Koranteng and Afua Manko
1967 T.O. Schandorf v. H.J.F. Schandorf

1968 Akyirem Bekoe v. Kofi Asante
1972 Bafour Gyekye Osei and another for themselves and the family v. Kwabena Bredu and three others
1973 Abena Agyaah v. Akua Addai and three others
Ankobea Ofori Sakyiama and others v. Obaapanyin Kumea and two others
1974 Daniel Kwadwo Danso v. Edward Kwadjo Appiah

KOFORIDUA HIGH COURT

1971 Opanin Daniel Appeakrong and Akosua Adae (Kwabeng) v. Ama Amoah and Akosua Anka (Kwabeng)
Yaw Frimpong v. Yaw Amanfo
Dora Osei v. Opanin Kofi Adu
Akua Brakoaa v. Grace Adofoaah and another
1972 Nana Oduro Ankobeah II v. Akua Adoma and Yaw Buobi
Alice Darkoaa and Yaa Seiwaa on behalf of three others v. Okwae Feming and Dede Akua
Madam Abena Poakwah v. Kwadwo Koto and Kwame Gyekye
Madam Agnes Agyeiwaa and children v. Kwame Adu
Ama Seiwaah v. Kofi Agyei
1973 Christian Forster Oteng substituted by Yaw Frempong v. Kwadjo Asimeng and Helena Akua Dakwa
Amma Donkor v. Kwame Oware and four others
Mrs Margaret Amakye v. Madam Christiana Donkor (Afua Nkrumah)
Akua Pokua v. Kofi Boateng
1974 Akua Asaabah per Kodjo Beng v. Kwadjo Amoah and another

KUMASI HIGH COURT

1963 Kwaku Agyekum v. Kwame Mensah
1964 Akua Saah v. Kwaku Sampane
1965 Kwaku Amoateng v. Akwasi Sekyere
1966 Akua Darkowaa v. Afua Mansah and seven others
1967 Kofi Nyame alias Kofi Ankama, Kojo Fordjour and Afua Sie v. Kofi Nyame Asiama, Yaw Budu and Afua Nyanese
1968 Kwame Kumah v. Kofi Moshie, Amma Donkor, Kwadwo Antwi and Kwaku Forkuo
Stephen Kwaku Aning and Christiana Yennowo v. Yaw Barimah
1969 Chief Kwadwo Asabere v. Thomas Kwao, E.K. Annoh, Kwasi Barima and Kojo Amuah
Akua Aboaa, Yaa Asantewaa v. Kwame Dapaa
Opanin Kojo Adu Amansa v. Opanin Kofi Asante and another
1970 Okyeame Kwaku Agyei v. Co-operative Union and another
Madam Agnes Ankonam and brothers and sisters v. P.S. Anhwere and another
Kofi Asare v. Akosua Twumwah and two others
Kwasi Agyei v. Nana Yaw Acheampong and two others
1971 Kwabena Sarkodie Ababio v. Philip Asante and two others
Akosua Akuaa v. Kwame Adiyia and two others
1972 Madam Akosua Addai v. Madam Akosua Bedabour and four others
Kwaku Adabanka v. Yaa Ntiriwaa
Kwasi Amadu v. Kwaku Sarfo

1974 Peter Antwi Sono v. Okomfo Yaa
Kwame Amponsah v. Yaw Barimah

SUNYANI HIGH COURT

1966 Case between sons and daughters and nephew as heir heard first 14 October 1966. Dispute around sharing of properties of deceased.
1967 Dispute between heirs first heard 16 January 1967.
1968 Amma Kumah v. Yaa Nkrumah and Kofi Krah
1969 Abenaa Appeah alias Abena Agyem v. Yaw Kumi alias Kyirifufuo
Comfort Dapaah v. Abena Amane
1970 Adwoa Fordwo v. Yaw Ampofo
Afua Manu v. Kwadwo Akwa
1971 Bosomfuor Kwabena Koranteng v. Abena Donkor
Case between uncle and nephew first heard 14 December 1971. Plaintiff suing on behalf of the family against nephew mortgaging property.
F.K. Boafo, E.K. Boafo, S.K. Boafo, E. Boafo v. Opanin Adu D. Kwadwo
Kwabena Donkor v. Kwadwu Afum and Amma Buruwaa
1972 Abena Nnuro, Kojo Nsowah, Kofi Adunan, Kwame Num v. Thomas Owusu
Case between members of the same family. Attempts to sell family property for debt settlement heard first 15 March 1972.
Sibling disputing with heir to half-brother. First heard 10 March 1972.
Paul Edward Nkrumah, Osahene Otiwaa and Mary Otiwaa v. Kwabena Num
Yaw Amoah v. Kofi Agyei
Afua Saase v. Kwame Yomuah and Opanin Kwabena
Kofi Antwi v. Adu Kwabena and Kwaku Akwan
Akosua Nyarko v. Kofi Mensah and Kojo Nyamesem
1973 Amma Nsiah for herself and on behalf of Kwadwo Ansu and Oppong Kwabena family v. Kwasi Sabi and Kwasi Biri
Case of an attempt to use family property for debt settlement first heard 10 January 1973.

CIRCUIT COURT KOFORIDUA

1963 Akwasi Sasu v. Koranteng and Kwaku Amoah
1964 Kwaku Antijyan v. Adwowa Sekyiwa
1969 Kwame Adu v. Agnes Agyeiwa and two others
1970 Martey Narh Kwaku v. Gabriel Kofi Kumah
Seth Nyarkoh v. Yaw Ampofo and another
1972 K. Adae v. A. Dentah and another
Akua Awusiba v. Kofi Boye and others
1974 Afua Appeah and another v. Emmanuel Oppong and another
Adjoa Akyaa and Yaw Sarfo v. Opanin Kwaku Sarpong

CIRCUIT COURT KUMASI

1970 Kwaku Forkuo v. Kwadwo Ntidwo
1971 Akosua Akwaa v. Kwame Adiyia, Kwasi Kufuor and Kae Dabi
1972 Opanin Kwasi Sikayena v. Madam Adwoa Addae and Barikese Co-operative Society
Kwame Korkor and others v. Kwame Krah
Opanin Kofi Agyim v. Madam Akua Tawiah
1973 Madam Akosua Badu v. Kwaku Ameyaw
Osei Akoto v. Kwabena Denteh and one other

CIRCUIT COURT SUNYANI

1968 Adwoa Korkor, Akosua Dankwah and Yaa Daagye v. Opanin Kwame Dada and Amma Adoma
Yaw Bogo v. Yaa Serwaah
Kwasi Boonyinah v. Yaa Serwaah
1969 Kwabena Kyereme v. Kwadwo Badu
1970 Adwoa Krah v. Kwaku Yeboah
Opanin Kwame Manu v. Kramo Aboohie
Madam Adwoa Mansah v. Opanyin Kwame Osei and Adwoa Aso
Opanyin Kofi Wusu v. Madam Abena Newanse
Adwoa Haawah v. Kramo Moro
Afua Ayaame v. Nana Oppong Yaw
Akosua Mansah, Akua Forkua, Yaa Saah and Kwabena Baah v. D.K. Yoboah and T.K. Obeng
Cecelia Akua Abrafi, John K. Owusu and five others v. Yaw Barimah
1971 Opanyin Kwadwo Waaye v. Kwame Dakwah, Yaw Addo, J.K. Yeboah and Kwadwo Nkrumah
Kwame Waye v. Akua Bisi
Yaw Korkor v. Kwame Kontor
Afua Fofie v. Kwame Kontor
1972 Rockson Adjei v. Madam Amma Kraah
Opanin Atta Kwabena v. Kramo Seidu
Kwadwo Manu v. Ama Rose
1973 Nana Kwadwo Opoku v. Yaw Krah
1974 Joseph Adu Alias Kwadwo Barnieh v. Isaac Berko and Samuel Berko

DISTRICT COURT GRADE I KOFORIDUA

1969 Madam Akua Duku v. Abana Gyamfua and Alfred Appiah Dankwah
1973 Atta Kofi v. Richard Ebenezer Kwaku Akyea
Kwabena Dapaah v. Kwaku Kuma

DISTRICT COURT GRADE I GOASO

1972 Afua Kunadu v. Yaa Kunadu and Kwaku Dwumo
Ama Kwartemaah v. Kofi Frimpong
Madam Afua Achiaa v. Madam Yaa Aboraa
Akua Amoanimah v. Kofi Antwi
Afua Mansah v. Kyere Nyame

1973 Abena Boadiwaah on behalf of her family v. Opanin Kofi Nsiah
Kojo Ntodi on behalf of the family v. Yaw Krah
Nana Kwame Nti per Ajoa Tawiah v. Yaw Biah
Adjoa Boah v. Kojo Boye
Lord Mohammed Akowua v. Alhasan Yaw Marfo
Amma Tawiah v. Kofi Nsowaah
Opanin Kofi Afrim v. Kwasi Kruko
J.A. Ashie Kwofie v. Kyere Nyame and Nana Edusei II
Kwaku Asiama v. Kwabena Aboko
Akua Kwatemaa v. Panin Owu-Akyir
A.K. Addae v. Kojo Boye
Kwasi Appiah v. Nana Kwasi Adu Yeboah
Yaw Ohunya v. Ashun Amanfo
Amma Badu on behalf of her children v. Emmanuel Akoto

Record of Land Cases

Name of court:........................ Year recorded........................

Name of plaintiff/s	
Name of defendant/s	
New case/on transfer	
If on transfer: date of first hearing	
Date of last hearing in this court	
Judgment given/struck out/ transferred/still in court/ on appeal	
Relationship of defendants to plaintiff/s	
Ethnic group of plaintiff/s/ defendants	
Plaintiff's (P) case	
Defendant's (D) case	

Appendix 4

Co-operative credit and block planting schemes in Ashanti

TABLE A4.1 Co-operative credit and block planting schemes

	Block planting schemes		Co-operative credit scheme
	Abosoma	Odumasi	Beposo
Number of farmers interviewed	15	17	34
Total farmers in scheme in 1973	16	18	57
Year scheme started-ended	1968-71	1968-71	1972-3
Final acreage involved	120	120	975[a]
Acreage range per farmer	0.4-40.0	0.7-10.0[b]	1.5-64.0

[a]This acreage covers loans given over two years. Thirty farmers received a loan in 1972 covering 231 acres, fifty-four in 1973 covering 744 acres. Twenty-five farmers received a loan in both years. Acreage for one farmer who received a loan in 1973 was not available.

[b]Acreage not calculated for eight plots. Acreage covered by remaining ten plots was 37.3

TABLE A4.2 Age distribution of farmers interviewed by sex and home town

	Home town		
	This locality	Another locality, same district	Another district, same region
Age in years			
Males			
25-44	10.8	12.5	-
45-64	51.4	50.0	20.0
65+	37.8	37.5	80.0
Total	100.0	100.0	100.0
Number of persons	37	8	5
Females			
25-44	6.7	-	-
45-64	80.0	-	-
65+	13.3	100.0	-
Total	100.0	100.0	-
Number of persons	15	1	
N = 66			

Interview Schedule

Name of farmer..........................Age..........Sex.............
Usual residence (place/district)....................................
Home town (place/district/region)...................................
Acreage included in:
credit scheme.................................
block planting scheme.........................
year planted..................................

COCOA FARMS

1 Can you tell me something about all your cocoa farms? (INCLUDING the one in the Credit/Block Planting Scheme) (Interviewer see separate sheet. Number all farms 1, 2, 3, etc.; mark with x the farm in the scheme.)
2 Which is the largest farm?
3 Which farm is your most important farm? Why is this your most important farm?
4 On which farm have you spent most money?
5 On which farm have you spent most time?
6 If you had money of your own would you consider investing money in existing farms?
Which farm?...
Starting another farm?..
Starting another business?....................................
Property investment?..
Why?

INFORMATION SOURCES - COCOA

7 Have you ever been to a cocoa station? Yes/No. If Yes, for what? Did you get what you wanted?
8 Have you ever sought information/inputs from any other official source? Yes/No. If Yes, where, and what did you want? Did you get what you wanted?

OTHER FARMS/LAND

9 Have you any farms other than those planted with cocoa? Yes/No. If Yes, where are they? (Place/district/region.) What crop/s are planted? Who looks after them?
10 Have you any 'abandoned' (no longer harvested) cocoa farms? Yes/No. If Yes, can you tell me something about them? Where are they? (Place/district/region.) Why are they abandoned? When were they abandoned? Were they already abandoned when you acquired them? How did you acquire them? If inherited, from whom? When did you acquire them? Have you ever considered replanting them? What do you consider to be the main problem preventing replanting?
11 Have you any land anywhere not planted with any crop? Yes/No.

If Yes, what do you intend to do with it? Where is it? How did you acquire it? When did you acquire it?

12 Do you look after any farms for anyone else? Yes/No. If Yes, what do you actually do? If Yes, can you tell me something about them? Whose farms are they? What crop is planted? Where is the owner? Do you get anything (money, goods) for doing this? Do you earn a larger income from them than from any of your own farms? How long have you been looking after them?

PERSONAL INFORMATION

13 Have you ever had or do you have at present (state which) another occupation other than farming? What? If Yes, but no longer having, why did you stop? Who looked after your farms while you were doing this work?

14(a) Have you ever assisted anyone on his/her cocoa farms both before and since you started on your own? Yes/No. If Yes, whose farms and what kind of assistance did you give? (b) What did you do before you acquired your own farms?

15 Did/or does your father have any cocoa farms? Yes/No. If Yes, who is looking after these now?

16 Can you tell me something about all your children?

Age	Sex	Occupation/school	Schooling - class reached
...	...	....	....

Who paid or is paying?.........................

Do any of your children have their own separate farms (cocoa or food)? If Yes, where are they? (Cocoa/food.) How did they acquire them? (Cocoa/food.)

For children in business: Who helped them to start? In what way did they/you help them?

17 Can you tell me something about your brothers and sisters? How many brothers and sisters have you?

	Same mother	Same father
Brothers	....	....
Sisters	....	....

Are any of them farming or in business on their own?

	Business no.	Farming no.	If farming, crop/s grown
Brothers Yes/No......			
Sisters Yes/No......			

If Yes, who helped them to start?

Brothers.........................

Sisters.........................

18 Male farmers:

Can you tell me something about your wife/wives? How many wives do you have at present? What is their occupation? Do they work jointly or separately from you?

Wife	Age	Occupation/s	Separate or joint with husband?	If farmer, what are they growing?	Where do they work?
....	...	....	....	....	....

For wives in separate business or with separate farms: Who helped them to start? In what way were they helped?

19 All farmers:
Have you ever provided money/farms for anyone (other than those already mentioned) to start in business of any kind? Yes/No. If Yes, who and for what purpose?

20 Apart from your farms, have you any other business/property? Yes/No. If Yes, what and how did you acquire or start it? When did you start or acquire it? If you have a business, who is working there? Where is your: (a) business; (b) property?

21 Did you go to school? Yes/No. If Yes, what class did you reach? Who paid?

22 Have you, or are you, paying for anyone's education other than those already mentioned? Yes/No. If Yes, for whom?

Question 1 Cocoa farms

Acreage (if known)

Where are they?
Place/district/region

When did you acquire them?

When were they first planted?

Have they ever been replanted? Yes/No
(Not filling vacancies.)
If Yes, by whom? When?

If planted self, who helped you to plant?

Where did you get your seeds/seedlings from?

What variety of cocoa is planted?

Which farm gives you the highest/next highest/ lowest income, etc.?

How many loads did you get last year (including caretaker's return)?

Main crop?

Mid crop?

Is the yield at present increasing/stable/ decreasing?

Apart from yourself, has anyone else ever invested in the farms? Who?
Time:
Money:

Who is looking after the farms now? (On site.)

If caretakers, are they related to you? (Note relationship.)

What do they receive for doing this?

If not looking after own farms, what work are you doing at present?

Do you share the proceeds with anyone? (Apart from caretakers.)

Who?

How did you acquire
these farms? (Purchase/
gift/inherited, etc.)

If purchase:
Purchased from whom?
What are the terms of
purchase?

How did you acquire
the money for purchase?

If gift inherited:
From whom did you acquire
them?

When you acquired them,
was the yield increasing/
decreasing/stable?

References

ADDO, N.O. (1972), Employment and Labour Supply on Ghana's Cocoa Farms in the Pre and Post Aliens Compliance Order Era, 'The Economic Bulletin of Ghana', second series, vol. 2, no. 4, pp. 33-50.
ADDO, N.O. (1974), Employment and Labour Conditions on Ghana's Cocoa Farms. In 'The Economics of Cocoa Production and Marketing', ed. R.A. Kotey, C. Okali and B.E. Rourke. Legon, Institute of Statistical, Social and Economic Research, pp. 204-18.
ADEGBOYE, R.O. and OKALI, C. (1975), Some Observations on the Eastern Region Cocoa Rehabilitation Project. An example of Government Participation in Agricultural Production in Ghana, 'Economic and Social Affairs', vol. 1, no. 4, pp. 2-10.
ADOMAKO-SARFOH, J. (1965), Brong-Ahafo Cocoa Farming, unpublished MA thesis for the Institute of African Studies, University of Ghana, Legon.
ADOMAKO-SARFOH, J. (1971), Migrant Asante Cocoa Farmers and Their Families, 'Legon Family Research Papers', no. 1, Institute of African Studies, University of Ghana, Legon, pp. 129-44.
ALDOUS, J. (1962), Urbanisation, The Extended Family and Kinship Ties in West Africa, 'Social Forces', vol. 41, no. 1, pp. 6-12.
ALLAN, W. (1965), 'The African Husbandman', Edinburgh, Oliver & Boyd.
APPIAH, A.S. (1970), The Organisation of Labour in the Production of Cocoa Beans: A Survey of Tepa District, unpublished BSc thesis for the Department of Agricultural Economics, University of Ghana, Legon.
ARHIN, K. ed. (1970), Collected Papers on Ahafo Landholding, 'Research Review', Supplement no. 3, Institute of African Studies, University of Ghana, Legon.
BARTH, F. (1967), On the Study of Social Change, 'American Anthropologist', vol. 69, no. 6, pp. 661-9.
BECKETT, W.H. (1947), Akokoaso, a Survey of a Gold Coast Village, 'Monographs on Social Anthropology', no. 10, London, Percy Lund Humphries for the London School of Economics.
BECKETT, W.H. (1972), Koransang Cocoa Farm 1904-1970, 'Technical Publication Series', no. 31, Legon, Institute of Statistical, Social and Economic Research.
BECKMAN, B. (1970), The Distribution of Cocoa Income, 1961-1965, paper presented at a seminar, Legon, Department of Economics.

BELSHAW, C.S. (1967), Reviewing Primitive and Peasant Economic Systems by M. Nash, 'Current Anthropology', no. 8, pp. 244-50.

BENNEH, G. (1970), The Impact of Cocoa Cultivation on the Traditional Land Tenure System of the Akan of Ghana, 'Ghana Journal of Sociology', vol. 6, no. 1, pp. 43-61.

BENNEH, G. (1971), Land Tenure and Sabala Farming System in the Anlo Area of Ghana, 'Research Review', vol. 7, no. 2, Legon, Institute of African Studies, pp. 74-94.

BENTSI-ENCHILL, K. (1964), Ghana Land Law: an exposition, analysis and critique, 'Law in Africa, no. 10', London, Sweet & Maxwell.

BERRY, S. (1975), 'Cocoa, Custom and Socio-economic Change in Rural Western Nigeria', Oxford, Clarendon Press.

BOATEN, K. (1974), Problems Facing Cocoa Farmers in Mampong, an Old Cocoa Growing District in Ashanti. In 'The Economics of Cocoa Production and Marketing', ed. R.A. Kotey, C. Okali and B.E. Rourke. Legon, Institute of Statistical, Social and Economic Research, pp. 196-203.

BOSERUP, E. (1970), 'Women's Role in Economic Development', London, George Allen & Unwin.

BOTT, E. (1971), 'Family and Social Network: Roles, Norms and External Relationships in Ordinary Urban Families', London, Tavistock Publications.

BROATCH, J.D. (1956), Problems of Cocoa Growing in the Gold Coast, 'New Gold Coast Farmer', vol. 1, no. 1, pp. 2-5.

BROKENSHA, D. (1966), 'Social Change at Larteh, Ghana', Oxford, Clarendon Press.

BUSIA, K.A. (1951), 'The Position of the Chief in the Modern Political System of the Ashanti', London, Oxford University Press for the International African Institute.

CALDWELL, J.C. (1968), 'Population Growth and Family Change in Ghana: The New Urban Elite in Ghana', Canberra, Australia National University Press.

CENSUS OFFICE (1931), '1930 Population Census of Ghana', Accra, Government Printer.

CENSUS OFFICE (1960), 1960 'Population Census of Ghana': vol. 11 Statistics of Localities and Enumeration Areas, Accra, Census Office.

CENSUS OFFICE (1964), 'Population Census of Ghana. Special Report "E" Tribes in Ghana', Accra, Census Office.

CENSUS OFFICE (1972), 1970 'Population Census of Ghana': vol. 11 Statistics of Localities and Enumeration Areas, Accra, Census Office.

COLLINGWOOD, C.A. (1972), Cocoa in West Africa; the Economics of Pest Control, 'Span', vol. 15, no. 2, p. 74.

COLSON, E. (1960), 'Social Organization of the Gwembe Tonga', Manchester, Manchester University Press.

DANQUAH, J.E. (1928), 'Akan Laws and Customs and the Akim Abuakwa Constitution', London, Routledge.

DOUGLAS, M. (1969), Is Matriliny Doomed in Africa? In 'Man in Africa', ed. M. Douglas and P.M. Kaberry. London, Tavistock Publications, pp. 121-36.

DUPIRE, M. (1971), The Position of Women in a Pastoral Society. The Fulani WoDaaBe, Nomads of the Niger. In 'Women of Tropical Africa', ed. D. Paulme. Berkeley, University of California Press, pp. 47-92.

EKEH, P.P. (1974), 'Social Exchange Theory. The Two Traditions', Cambridge, Mass., Harvard University Press.
EPSTEIN, T.S. (1967), 'Economic Development and Social Change in South India', Manchester, Manchester University Press.
FIELD, M.J. (1960), 'Search for Security: An Ethno-psychiatric Study of Rural Ghana', London, Faber.
FORDE, D. (1950), Double Descent Among the Yako. In 'African Systems of Kinship and Marriage', ed. A.R. Radcliffe-Brown and D. Forde. London, Oxford University Press for the International African Institute, pp. 285-332.
FORTES, M. (1948), The Ashanti Social Survey: A Preliminary Report, 'Rhodes Livingstone Journal', no. 6, pp. 1-36.
FORTES, M. (1950), Kinship and Marriage Among the Ashanti. In 'African Systems of Kinship and Marriage', ed. A.R. Radcliffe-Brown and D. Forde. London, Oxford University Press for the International African Institute, pp. 252-84.
FORTES, M. (1953), The Structure of Unilineal Descent Groups, 'American Anthropologist', vol. 55, no. 1, pp. 17-41.
FORTES, M. (1970), Time and Social Structure: An Ashanti Case Study. In 'Time and Social Structure and other Essays'. London, The Athlone Press.
FORTES, M. (1971), 'The Family: Bane or Blessing?' An open lecture delivered at the University of Ghana, Legon, 3 March 1971, Accra, Ghana Universities Press.
FORTES, M. (1973), Preface to Inter-state Boundary Litigation in Ashanti by A.A.Y. Kyerematen, 'African Social Research Documents', vol. 4, Cambridge, African Studies Center, pp. v-x.
FORTES, M. (1975), Strangers. In 'Studies in African Social Anthropology', ed. M. Fortes and S. Patterson. London, Academic Press.
FRANKENBERG, R. (1967), Economic Anthropology: One Anthropologist's View. In 'Themes in Economic Anthropology', ed. R. Firth. London, Tavistock Publications, pp. 47-89.
GALLETTI, R., BALDWIN, K.D.S. and DINA, I.O. (1956), 'Nigerian Cocoa Farmers: An Economic Survey of Yoruba Cocoa Farming Families', London, Oxford University Press.
GARLICK, P.C. (1971), 'African Traders and Economic Development in Ghana', Oxford, Clarendon Press.
GCMB (n.d.), 'Hints for Cocoa Farmers', 2nd edn, Accra, Ghana Cocoa Marketing Board.
GHANA, MINISTRY OF AGRICULTURE (1972), 'Report on Ghana Sample Census of Agriculture: vol. 1', Accra, Economics and Marketing Division.
GOODE, W.J. (1963), 'World Revolution and Family Patterns', New York, Free Press of Glencoe.
GOODY, J. (1958), The Fission of Domestic Groups Among the LoDagaba. In 'The Development Cycle in Domestic Groups', ed. J. Goody. Cambridge, Cambridge University Press, pp. 53-91.
GOODY, J. (1962), 'Death, Property and the Ancestors: A Study of the Mortuary Customs of the LoDagaba of West Africa', London, Tavistock Publications.
GOODY, J. (1965), Descent Groups. Article for the 'Encyclopaedia of the Social Sciences', Legon, Institute of African Studies.
GOODY, J. (1969), Inheritance, Property and Marriage in Africa and Eurasia, 'Sociology', vol. 3, no. 1, pp. 55-76.

GOODY, J. (1970), Marriage Presentations, Inheritance and Descent in Pre-industrial Societies, 'Journal of Comparative Family Studies', vol. 1, no. 1.

GOUGH, K. (1952), Changing Kinship Usages in the Setting of Political and Economic Change Among the Nayars of Malabar, 'Journal of the Royal Anthropological Institute', vol. 82, pp. 71-88.

GOUGH, K. (1961), Variations in Interpersonal Kinship Relationships. In 'Matrilineal Kinship', ed. D.M. Schneider and K. Gough. Berkeley, University of California Press, pp. 577-613.

GRAY, R.F. and GULLIVER, P.H. eds (1964), 'The Family Estate in Africa: Studies in the Role of Property in Family Structure and Lineage Continuity', London, Routledge & Kegan Paul.

HANDWERKER, W.P. (1973), Kinship, Friendship and Business Failure Among Market Sellers in Monrovia, Liberia, 1970, 'Africa', vol. XLIII, no. 4, pp. 288-301.

HILL, P. (1962), Social Factors in Cocoa Farming. In 'Agriculture and Land Use in Ghana', ed. J.B. Wills. London, Oxford University Press for the Ghana Ministry of Food and Agriculture, pp. 278-85.

HILL, P. (1963), 'The Migrant Cocoa Farmers of Southern Ghana: A Study in Rural Capitalism', Cambridge, Cambridge University Press.

HOPEN, C.E. (1958), 'The Pastoral Fulbe Family in Gwandu', London, Oxford University Press for the International African Institute.

HUNTER, J.M. (1961), Akotuakrom: A Case Study of a Devastated Cocoa Village in Ghana, 'Transactions and Papers of the Institute of British Geographers', no. 29, pp. 161-86.

JIBOWU, O. (Chairman) (1956), 'Report of the Commission of Enquiry into the Management and Organisation of the Cocoa Purchasing Company Limited', Accra, Government Printer.

KILLICK, T. (1966), Labour: A General Survey. In 'A Study of Contemporary Ghana; vol. 1 The Economy of Ghana', ed. W. Birmingham, I. Neustadt and E.N. Omaboe. London, George Allen & Unwin.

KOTEY, R.A. (1972), Competition Between Cocoa and Coffee, A Case Study, 'Technical Publication Series', no. 29, Legon, Institute of Statistical, Social and Economic Research.

KOTEY, R.A., OKALI, C. and ROURKE, B.E. eds (1974), 'The Economics of Cocoa Production and Marketing', Legon, Institute of Statistical, Social and Economic Research.

KYEREMATEN, A.A.Y. (1973), Inter-state Boundary Litigation in Ashanti, 'African Social Research Documents', vol. 4, Cambridge, African Studies Center.

LANFRANCHI, J. (1962), Cocoa Growing and Production Costs on African Farms in the Ivory Coast. In 'Report of the Cocoa Conference', London, 1961. London, The Cocoa Chocolate and Confectionary Alliance, pp. 66-74.

LESTON, D. (1974), The Diseconomy of Insecticides in Cocoa Production in Ghana. In 'The Economics of Cocoa Production and Marketing', ed. R.A. Kotey, C. Okali and B.E. Rourke. Legon, Institute of Statistical, Social and Economic Research, pp. 96-104.

LITTLE, K. (1959), Some Urban Patterns of Marriage and Domesticity in West Africa, 'Sociological Review', new series, vol. 7, no. 1, pp. 65-82.

LLOYD, P.C. ed. (1966), 'The New Elites of Tropical Africa', London, Oxford University Press for the International African Institute.

LONG, N. (1968), 'Social Change and the Individual. A Study of the

Social and Religious Responses to Innovation in a Zambian Rural Community', Manchester, University Press for the Institute of Social Research, University of Zambia.
MARWICK, M.G. (1965), 'Sorcery in Its Social Setting. A Study of the Northern Rhodesia Cewa', Manchester, Manchester University Press.
MAUSS, M. (1974), 'The Gift: Forms and Functions of Exchange in Archaic Societies', London, Routledge & Kegan Paul.
MEEK, C.K. (1957), 'Land Tenure and Land Administration in Nigeria and the Cameroons', Colonial Research Studies, no. 22, London, HMSO.
NOWELL, W. (Chairman) (1938), 'Report of the Commission on the Marketing of West African Cocoa', London, HMSO.
OKALI, C. (1975), Dominase. A Mobile Cocoa Farming Community in Brong Ahafo, 'Technical Publication Series', no. 35, Legon, Institute of Statistical, Social and Economic Research.
OKALI, C. and ADDY, P.N.L.A. (1974), 'Economics of Cocoa Production and Marketing with Special Reference to Ghana. An Annotated Bibliography', Legon, Institute of Statistical, Social and Economic Research.
OKALI, C. and KOTEY, R.A. (1971), Akokoaso: A Resurvey, 'Technical Publication Series', no. 15, Legon, Institute of Statistical, Social and Economic Research.
OKALI, C. and MABEY, S.Y. (1974), Women in Agriculture in Southern Ghana, 'Manum', vol. 8, no. 2, pp. 13-40.
OKALI, C., GYEKYE, L.O. and MABEY, S.Y. (1975), 'Report on the Socio-economic Characteristics of the Ashanti Cocoa Rehabilitation Area', Technical report prepared for the Ghana Cocoa Marketing Board, Legon, Institute of Statistical, Social and Economic Research.
OLLENNU, N.A. (1959), Judgement in the case of Quartey v Martey and Anor, 'Ghana Law Report', p. 377.
OLLENNU, N.A. (1962), 'Principles of Customary Land Law in Ghana', London, Sweet & Maxwell.
OPPONG, C. (1970), Aspects of Conjugal Relationships Among Akan Senior Civil Servants in Accra, Cambridge PhD thesis.
OPPONG, C. (1972), Norms and Variations: A Study of Ghanaian Students' attitudes to Marriage and Family Living, 'Legon Family Research Papers', no. 3, Legon, Institute of African Studies.
PARKIN, D.J. (1972), 'Palms, Wine and Witness. Public Spirit and Private Gain in an African Farming Community', London, Intertext Book Co.
QUAIDOO, P.K. (Chairman) (1956), 'Report of the Committee on Agricultural Indebtedness', Accra, Government Printer.
RADCLIFFE-BROWN, A.R. (1950), 'Introduction to African Systems of Kinship and Marriage', ed. A.R. Radcliffe-Brown and D. Forde. London, Oxford University Press for the International African Institute, pp. 1-85.
RATTRAY, R.S. (1923), 'Ashanti', Oxford, Clarendon Press.
RATTRAY, R.S. (1929), 'Ashanti Law and Constitution', Oxford, Clarendon Press.
RICHARDS, A.I. (1939), 'Land, Labour and Diet in Northern Rhodesia. An Economic Study of the Bemba Tribe', London, Oxford University Press for the International African Institute.
RICHARDS, A.I. (1951), The Bemba of North-Eastern Rhodesia. In 'Seven Tribes of British Central Africa', ed. E. Colson and M.

Gluckman. London, Oxford University Press for the Rhodes Livingstone Institute, pp. 207-51.

ROBERTSON, A.F. (1973), Histories and Political Opposition in Ahafo, Ghana, 'Africa', vol. XLIII, no. 1, pp. 41-58.

ROURKE, B.E. (1971), Wages and Incomes of Agricultural Workers in Ghana, 'Technical Publication Series', no. 13, Legon, Institute of Statistical, Social and Economic Research.

ROURKE, B.E. (1974), Profitability of Cocoa and Alternative Crops in Eastern Region, Ghana. In 'The Economics of Cocoa Production and Marketing', ed. R.A. Kotey, C. Okali and B.E. Rourke, Legon, Institute of Statistical, Social and Economic Research, pp. 20-46.

SAHLINS, M. (1972), 'Stone Age Economics', Chicago, Aldine, Atherton Inc.

SARBAH, J.M. (1897), 'Fanti Customary Laws', London, Clowes.

SCHNEIDER, D.M. (1961), 'Introduction to Matrilineal Kinship', ed. D.M. Schneider and K. Gough. Berkeley, University of California Press.

SCHNEIDER, D.M. and GOUGH, K. eds (1961), 'Matrilineal Kinship', Berkeley, University of California Press.

SCHNEIDER, H.K. (1974a), 'Economic Man: The Anthropology of Economics', New York, The Free Press.

SCHNEIDER, H.K. (1974b), Development and Economic Change: The Case of East African Cattle, 'Current Anthropology', vol. 15, no. 3, pp. 259-65.

SELLTIZ, C., JAHODA, M., DEUTSCH, M. and COOK, S.W. (1962), 'Research Methods in Social Relations', London, Methuen for the Society for the Psychological Study of Social Issues.

SHEPHERD, C.Y. (1936), Report on the Economics of Peasant Agriculture in the Gold Coast, 'Gold Coast Sessional Papers', no. 1, Accra, Government Printer.

SIMMS, R.P. (1965), 'Urbanisation in West Africa: A Review of Current Literature', Evanston, North-western University Press.

SMYTHE, H.H. and SMYTHE, M.M. (1960), 'The New Nigerian Elite', Stanford, Stanford University Press.

SOUTHALL, A.W. ed. (1961), 'Social Change in Modern Africa', London, Oxford University Press.

TURNER, V.W. (1957), 'Schism and continuity in an African Society, A Study of Ndembu Village Life', Manchester, Manchester University Press.

UCHENDU, V.C. (1969), Field Study of Agricultural Change: The Cocoa Farmers of Akim Abuakwa, Eastern Region, Ghana, 'Economic, Cultural and Technical Determinants of Agricultural Changes in Africa', Preliminary Report no. 8, Food Research Institute, Stanford University.

UNESCO (1956), 'Social Implications of Industrialisation and Urbanisation of Africa South of the Sahara', London, International African Institute.

VAN DE GEEST, S. (1974), Family Dynamics in a Changing Society. A Case of a Rural Ghanaian Community, unpublished MSc thesis for the Department of Sociology, University of Ghana, Legon.

VERCRUIJSSE, E.V.W. (1972), The Dynamics of Fanti Domestic Organisation. A Comparison with Fortes' Ashanti Survey, 'Research Report Series', paper no. 12, Cape Coast, University of Cape Coast Social Studies Project.

WATSON, A. (Chairman) (1948), 'Report of the Commission of Enquiry into Disturbances in the Gold Coast', London, HMSO.

WOODMAN, G.R. (1966), 'The Development of Customary Land Law in Ghana', Cambridge, University of Cambridge.

Index